Cambridge Elements

Elements in Ancient East Asia
IDEAS: Religion and Philosophy, and the Arts and Sciences
edited by
Erica Fox Brindley
Pennsylvania State University
Rowan Kimon Flad
Harvard University

MIND AND PSYCHOLOGY IN EARLY CHINA

Lisa Raphals
University of California, Riverside

Shaftesbury Road, Cambridge CB2 8EA, United Kingdom

One Liberty Plaza, 20th Floor, New York, NY 10006, USA

477 Williamstown Road, Port Melbourne, VIC 3207, Australia

314–321, 3rd Floor, Plot 3, Splendor Forum, Jasola District Centre,
New Delhi – 110025, India

103 Penang Road, #05–06/07, Visioncrest Commercial, Singapore 238467

Cambridge University Press is part of Cambridge University Press & Assessment,
a department of the University of Cambridge.

We share the University's mission to contribute to society through the pursuit of
education, learning and research at the highest international levels of excellence.

www.cambridge.org
Information on this title: www.cambridge.org/9781009669450

DOI: 10.1017/9781009298339

© Lisa Raphals 2025

This publication is in copyright. Subject to statutory exception and to the provisions
of relevant collective licensing agreements, no reproduction of any part may take
place without the written permission of Cambridge University Press & Assessment.

When citing this work, please include a reference to the DOI 10.1017/9781009298339

First published 2025

A catalogue record for this publication is available from the British Library

ISBN 978-1-009-66945-0 Hardback
ISBN 978-1-009-29832-2 Paperback
ISSN 2632-7325 (online)
ISSN 2632-7317 (print)

Cambridge University Press & Assessment has no responsibility for the persistence
or accuracy of URLs for external or third-party internet websites referred to in this
publication and does not guarantee that any content on such websites is, or will remain,
accurate or appropriate.

For EU product safety concerns, contact us at Calle de José Abascal, 56, 1°, 28003
Madrid, Spain, or email eugpsr@cambridge.org

Mind and Psychology in Early China

Elements in Ancient East Asia

DOI: 10.1017/9781009298339
First published online: December 2025

Lisa Raphals
University of California, Riverside
Author for correspondence: Lisa Raphals, lisa.raphals@ucr.edu

Abstract: This Element describes early Chinese views of the heart-mind (xin 心) and its relation to the psychology of a whole person, including the body, affective and cognitive faculties, and the spirit (shén 神). It argues for a divergence in Warring States thought between "mind-centered" and "spirit-centered" approaches to self-cultivation. It surveys the Analects, Mengzi, Guanzi, Zhuangzi, Xunzi, Huainanzi, the Huangdi neijing, and excavated medical manuscripts from Mawangdui, as well as a brief comparative perspective to ancient Greek views of these topics. It argues for a contrast between post-Cartesian dualism and Chinese and Greek psycho-physicalism.

Keywords: Embodiment, Mind (heart-mind, xin 心), Mind-Body problem, Psychology, Spirit (shén 神)

© Lisa Raphals 2025

ISBNs: 9781009669450 (HB), 9781009298322 (PB), 9781009298339 (OC)
ISSNs: 2632-7325 (online), 2632-7317 (print)

Contents

1 Introduction   1
2 Mind-Centered Texts   11
3 Spirit-Centered Perspectives   23
4 Medical Texts   36
5 Perspectives on Embodiment   48
6 Comparative Observations   51
7 Conclusions   56

References   59

1 Introduction

This Element describes early Chinese views of the mind and how it relates to the psychology of a whole person. In particular, it examines differing early views on the relation of the mind or heart-mind (*xin* 心) to affective and cognitive faculties, and to the spirit (*shén* 神) and the embodied person (*shēn* 身). A distinctive feature of Chinese philosophy is its recognition of the importance of the body and emotions in extensive and diverse self-cultivation traditions. It thus contrasts with Western philosophical debates about the relationship between mind and body, which are often described in terms of mind-body dualism. Questions of how our bodies relate to our minds or spirits are of central importance to several humanistic and scientific disciplines. The problem of mind–body dualism is central to the history of philosophy and religion; and recent work in cognitive and neuroscience underscores the importance of somatic experience for how we think and feel.[1]

There are multiple varieties of dualism, as well as multiple mind–body problems. For example, the term *dualism* refers to claims that, for a given domain, there are two fundamental kinds or categories of things or principles (e.g., Good and Evil in theology), in contrast to monism: the theory that there is only one fundamental principle, kind, or category of thing. (It also contrasts with pluralism: the view that there are many kinds or principles, kinds or categories.) In philosophy of mind, dualism refers to the theory that the mental and physical, or mind and body (including the brain) are composed of metaphysically different kinds of entities in that the former are nonmaterial and the latter material. The mind-body problem refers to problems of the relationship between mind and body, or between the mental and the physical. It includes: the ontological problem of distinguishing mental states from physical states and the nature of their relationship; causal questions of their mutual influence (if any); and related issues involving the nature of consciousness, intentionality, the self, and so on (Robinson 2017). I will focus on two of these: the (non)materiality of the mind and the relation between mental and physical states.

Parts of the Element summarize, in much compressed form, earlier research on the relation of body, mind, and spirit in early China (Raphals 2023). This Element differs from that earlier research in several ways. Most importantly, it focuses on the role of what in contemporary terms are called embodiment and embodied cognition (these terms are discussed in Section 5) in the philosophical traditions of early China. In addition, it offers brief comparative observations on the (perhaps, to some) surprising importance of embodied cognition in the world of ancient and Classical Greece.

---

[1] Eg., Damasio 1994 and 2010, Gallagher 2005, Johnson 1993.

1.1 Mind–Body Dualism and Its Problems

Mind–body dualism has become an important issue in Chinese and comparative philosophy because of claims that Chinese thought is in some sense "holist." There are various versions of this view. One is the claim that there was no mind–body dualism in early China; another takes the form of contrasts between supposed Chinese holism and "Western" dualism. These holist views tend to minimize distinctions between body and mind and spirit by reducing all three to material or quasi-material substances, often identified with *qi* 氣.[2] Dualist views – in the sense of mind–body dualism – have been historically Eurocentric. However, recent claims for concepts of mind–body dualism in early China argue against the holist position in a Chinese context. Arguments for mind–body dualism in a Chinese context make the claim that are part of a broader critique of a "neo-Orientalist" tendency to portray Chinese and Western thought as radically different. In particular, a series of studies by Edward Slingerland (Slingerland 2013, 2016, 2019) argue against claims that early China had no concept of mind–body dualism. This debate has led to renewed interest in the role of mind–body interactions in early Chinese thought. However, in a Chinese context, the "mind–body" binary encounters a problem: namely, the very important role of "spirit" (*shén*) and its relation to the mind.

In this Element I argue that there was an important divergence in early China between two views of the self. I begin with evidence that in early China there were two very different views of a person, understood as composed of body, mind, and spirit. In one, which can be called a mind-centered view, mind and spirit are closely aligned, and are understood to rule the body as a ruler rules a state or populace, in a hierarchically superior relation to the body. A polarity between body and mind/spirit (*xin/shén*) implies that mind and spirit are distinct from the body (for example, by being composed of a more refined kind of *qi* than the rest of the body). We see this view in the *Analects*, *Mengzi*, *Xunzi*, and tests excavated from Guodian. This view is very compatible with Eurocentric mind–body dualism.

In a very different spirit-centered view, all three were distinct, often with pride of place given to spirit over mind. In this view, the person is tripartite, and mind and spirit are independent entities that cannot be reduced to a material–non-material binary. In some cases body and spirit are even aligned in opposition to mind. This spirit-centered view rejects the hegemony of mind and gives

---

[2] *Qi* is one of several terms in Chinese philosophy that are impossible to translate and which I leave untranslated. *Qi* means something like "matter energy stuff" that constitutes our bodies and the material world. Dualist arguments do not squarely address the question of whether mind and spirit are material and composed of *qi*.

pride of place to spirit, sometimes in alliance with the body. Examples occur in the "Inner Workings" chapter of the *Guanzi*, the *Zhuangzi*, texts excavated from Mawangdui 馬王堆, and the *Huainanzi*.

1.1.1 Care of the Self

Several important studies have contributed to new understandings of the relations of body, mind, and spirit in early China. Some approaches discuss something analogous to what Foucault has called "the care of the self," better understood in a Chinese context as "self-cultivation" (*xiushēn* 修身) or "nurturing life" (*yangsheng* 養生). Self-cultivation traditions fundamentally involve the care and preservation of body, mind and spirit, but often disagree about relations between them. Some recent studies emphasize the importance of embodied self-cultivation traditions, from very different points of view.[3]

Michael Puett argues for a fundamental change in Chinese understandings of the relation between humans and gods, beginning in the fourth century BCE. At this time, critics of court sacrificial practices argued that humans could use self-cultivation practices to appropriate the powers of spirits, in effect to "become" spirits. As a result, the term *shén* – spirit(s) – came to include not only extrahuman spirits with powers over natural phenomena but also "spirit" capacities within humans, achieved through the refinement of *qi* within humans (Puett 2002: 21–23, 80–224).

Why did Warring States thinkers begin to claim that they could "become" spirits? According to Puett, Bronze Age attitudes toward spirits were fundamentally agonistic because spirits were capricious; sacrificial rituals were used to control them by transforming ancestors into gods in a divine hierarchy that was amenable to human manipulation through prayer and sacrifice (Puett 2002: 31–79, cf. Keightley 1978, 1998; Poo 1998). Warring States thinkers argued against these attitudes and effectively used the self-cultivation practices they advocated to reduce the distance between humans and gods. Such "self-divinization" practices increased individual human control and reduced the importance of divination and sacrifice.[4]

In a very different approach to self-cultivation, Edward Slingerland argues for the centrality of *wuwei* 無為 or "acting without acting" as a spiritual ideal for thinkers as diverse as Confucius, Mengzi, the authors of the *Daodejing*, *Zhuangzi*, and *Xunzi*. Slingerland describes *wuwei* as both a mental state

---

[3] For example see Lewis 2006, Sivin 1995, Wu 1997. For studies in Chinese see Yang 1993, 1999, and Zhang 2008.
[4] This approach offers new understandings of self-cultivation practices described in the *Neiye* and "Arts of the Mind" chapters of the *Guanzi*, the *Mengzi, and* the *Zhuangzi*, among others. See Puett 2002: 109–140, 170–172, and 202–224.

(characterized by effortlessness and lack of self-consciousness) and a mode of efficacious action (efficacious because it is in accord with the normative order of the cosmos) (Slingerland 2003b: 5, 7, 29–33). He considers *wuwei* central to a worldview in which the cosmos has a normative order, but humans have fallen away from their proper roles and modes of behavior. A person who has regained this original state through *wuwei* acquires power or charismatic virtue (*de* 德), but, paradoxically, "effortless action" can only be accomplished through self-cultivation characterized by the need to "try not to try."

Mark Csikszentmihalyi uses the *Mengzi* and two versions of the *Wuxing* 五行 ("Five Kinds of Action") recovered from Guodian 郭店 and Mawangdui 馬王堆 (Changsha, Hunan, c.168 BCE) to argue for what he calls a "material virtue" tradition: a detailed moral psychology that describes procedures for the cultivation of virtue(s) (Csikszentmihalyi 2005: 7). In particular, they describe virtues in terms similar to bodily humors. Csikszentmihalyi argues these texts describe sagehood in terms of material virtue; and that this "material virtue" tradition was a Ru ("Confucian") response to criticisms of the adequacy of "archaic" rituals for self-cultivation or the creation of social order.

In this material virtue tradition, virtue was grounded in the transformation of *qi*. It manifested physically in the body, and was inseparable from it. Cultivation of the virtues transforms the body and its appearance: it manifests in a jadelike countenance and the appearance of the eyes. This view of *qi* draws on late Warring States physiognomy and medicine. Medical and physiognomic texts share the view that internal *qi* is reflected in appearance and makes it possible to judge character or potential. In economic and military contexts this meant judging the "character" of an animal or weapon. Excavated texts show the importance of physiognomy in practical contexts. Examples include a text from Yinqueshan on the physiognomizing of dogs, a Han sword physiognomy text from Juyan and a text on the physiognomy of horses from Mawangdui.

These ethically normative self-cultivation traditions are important for several reasons. All involve body, mind, and spirit, often not clearly distinguished or explicitly blended. They provide strong expressions of "individualism" in early China, insofar as only an individual can perform self-cultivation (*xiushēn*) or "nurture life" (*yangsheng*). Only individuals can "*xiu*" their "*shēn*" or "*yang*" their "*sheng*." Most important for the purposes of this Element, they all involve knowledge that is embodied in the immediate sense that it is gained through physical practices. These approaches thus place the study of the body squarely within the purview of ethics. (A full account of issues of individualism is beyond the scope of the present discussion. See Brindley 2010.)

1.1.2 Arguments for Dualism

Several recent studies have argued for the importance of dualist views in early China (Graham 1989: 25, cf. Goldin 2003: 232, 243n22). Paul Goldin argued for the presence of mind–body dualism several of the most philosophically important Warring States texts. He points to passages in the *Zhuangzi* that seem to suggest the possibility of an immaterial mind or spirit, a passage in the *Xunzi* that presents a contrast between bodily and mental state, and Chinese beliefs about ghosts and postmortem consciousness (Goldin 2003: 228, 231, 2015).

In a recent monograph and several shorter studies, Edward Slingerland argues forcefully for the presence and importance of dualism in early China, and considers mind–body dualism to be one of several reductionist "Chinese-Western" dichotomies (Western dualism vs Chinese holism, Slingerland and Chudek 2011; critique by Klein and Klein 2012). Slingerland (2013: 9–15) argues against what he takes as the strongly holist positions of Roger Ames (1984, 1993), François Jullien (2007: 8, 69), and Herbert Fingarette (1972, 2008), among others. He argues for "weak" mind–body dualism, both in early China and as a psychological universal. He argues that in Chinese weak mind–body dualism, mind and body are experienced as functionally and qualitatively distinct, although potentially overlapping at points (Slingerland 2013: 28).

Slingerland's arguments also draw heavily on longstanding Chinese beliefs about the status of the soul after death. Chinese belief in some form of consciousness of the dead dates to the Shang oracle bone inscriptions; and Slingerland argues that, despite earlier evidence of belief in continuity between the world of the living and the dead, in late Warring States views of the afterlife, the dead were viewed as categorically different from the living (Guo 2011: 85–87; G. Lai 2005: 42; Slingerland 2019: 66–75).

He further argues that pre-Qin writers described the heart-mind or *xin* as the locus of personal identity, thought, free will, and moral responsibility, and as qualitatively different from other parts of the self (Slingerland 2019: 101). Finally, he argues that soul–body dualism was strongly developed by the third century BCE, including detailed accounts of ritual and religious techniques for freeing the mind/spirit from the body.[5]

Finally, Slingerland argues that any tripartite or multipartite account of the constituents of a person are "parasitic" on mind-body dualism because they all require the separability of personal essence from the physical body. (It also requires a close association between *shén* and the cognitive functions of *xin*.) He concludes that "if there is a unifying feature behind this diversity of terminology

---

[5] It could be argued that these definitions of dualism are too weak to be meaningful, and would be acceptable to most physicalists. I am grateful to an anonymous reader for pointing this out.

and divisions, it is that the soul ... is intimately bound up with consciousness or mind" (Slingerland 2019: 90). He argues that the unifying thread in a complex range of accounts of body-soul relations is

> a bipartite division between the dumb, concrete vessel that is the physical body and then a thing or collection of things that fill or inhabit this vessel. The latter serve as the locus/ loci of consciousness, intention, and personal identity. In other words, soul-body dualism (or tripartite-ism, decipartite-ism, etc.) is fundamentally parasitic on mind- body dualism. (Slingerland 2019: 92)

A dualist account of early Chinese psychology faces several problems. First, Chinese dualist arguments set up a problematic "body–mind" binary that conflates "mind–body" dualism and "spirit–body" dualism into one material–non-material binary that is historically Eurocentric. Second, most studies of mind–body dualism in early China are either not comparative or anachronistically compare early Chinese texts with modern European philosophers. Third, a dualist framework accounts for some of Chinese texts, but excludes others. Most broadly Confucian texts tend to identify the heart-mind with spirit and are thus friendly to this framework of analysis. But others present very separate roles of "mind" and "spirit."

Finally, the dualist position and the comparative "mind–body dualism" debate on which it draws rely on Western conceptual categories based on a Western "mind–body" binary. Most studies of "mind–body dualism" in early China collapse mind and spirit into one entity, which can be dualistically contrasted to the body, for example, in metaphors of the heart-mind as ruler of the body. Others tacitly equate mind–body dualism during life with body–spirit dualism after death, and result in alternating treatments of "mind–body" and "body–spirit" dualisms.

1.2 Mind- and Spirit-Centered Texts

None of these frameworks account for significant interactions between mind and spirit. A dualist framework of analysis loses important dimensions of the relations between mind (and its associated faculties) and spirit or soul (and its associated faculties), including how both relate to the body. I argue instead that Warring States texts present a broad divergence between two views of a tripartite relation between body, mind and spirit. One closely aligns mind and spirit, often in a hierarchically superior relation to the body; the other decouples spirit from mind, and at times even aligns body and spirit in opposition to mind.

The French Sinologist Catherine Despeux rejects dominant contemporary Western representations of persons as a dichotomy between body (corps) and mind (esprit), noting that questions of body and mind are typically the purview of philosophy, whereas the study of the psyche (psyché) is the purview of the disciplines of religion and even psychology. She understands the term *shén* as soul (l'âme, rather than "spirit") and proposes a tripartite representation of a person consisting of body, mind, and soul (a view she attributes to Greek thought, Aristotle's *On the Soul* especially):

> It seems desirable to get out of this dichotomy to analyze the vision in ancient China, especially since Western ancient thought most often referred to the trilogy body/soul/mind [corps/âme/esprit] which accords well enough with the analysis of subject and its components in Chinese culture. The Chinese equivalents of *xing* for the body, *shén* for the soul and *xin* for the heart/mind are easily found in body/soul/spirit. (Despeux 2007: 72)

I argue that there is a broad divergence between two views of a tripartite relation between body, mind, and spirit in Warring States texts. A mind-centered view aligns mind and spirit in a hierarchically superior relation to the body. A spirit-centered view problematizes the relation between mind and spirit, and in some cases even aligns body and spirit in opposition to mind. In this tripartite model, the self or person is composed of body in several aspects (including the form (*xing* 形), frame (*ti* 體), and embodied person (*shēn* 身, all discussed in detail in Section 1.3), the mind or heart-mind (*xin*) and the spirit (*shén*).

The mind-centered view closely aligns the heart-mind and spirit in a hierarchically superior relation to the body; together, they rule the body as ruler rules the people or a state. The result is effectively a binary view of a person – consistent with mind-body dualism – in which there is a polarity between the body on the one hand and mind and spirit on the other. Views of the heart-mind as ruler of the body, senses, and emotions changed over time; and this view is most prominent in the *Xunzi* but also appears to varying degrees in the *Guanzi*, *Mengzi*, *Huainanzi*, and *Huangdi neijing*.

The spirit-centered view gives pride of place to spirit (*shén*), both as the animating force that makes life possible and as the source of sagacity. In strong versions of the spirit-centered view, spirit is distinct from, superior to, and even at odds with the heart-mind, often operating through the body. This view is especially prominent in the *Zhuangzi* and the *Huainanzi*.

1.3 The Chinese Semantic Field

The Chinese semantic field for body, mind, and spirit differs from the English. No one term corresponds to either English "body," "mind," or "spirit." "Bodies" are described as frame (*ti* 體), form (*xing* 形), or embodied person (*shēn* 身). The term *xin* 心 or "heart-mind" refers to both the "mind" and the heart. The term *shén* 神 refers to both an internal capacity of humans and to "spirits," in the sense of divine powers external to humans.

1.3.1 Bodies: Frames and Forms

As important studies by Nathan Sivin and Deborah Sommer have demonstrated, Chinese terms for body have important differences from the English lexicon. They identify four key terms: *ti* 體, the physical body; *xing* 形, its structural form; *gong* 躬, the ritual person; and *shēn* 身, the social and self-cultivated person (Sivin 1995, Sommer 2008).

The *ti* or *frame* referred to the concrete physical body, including its major parts – usually the four limbs (*si ti* 四體) – and its physical form. An example of *ti* comes from Mengzi (2A2), who clearly refers to the entire body when he attributes to Gaozi a view of the body (*ti*) in which

> The will is the master of the *qi*; *qi* is what fills the frame. Where the will arrives, the *qi* comes after it. Therefore it is said; Take hold of your will and do not do violence to the *qi*.
>
> 夫志, 氣之帥也; 氣, 體之充也。夫志至焉, 氣次焉。故曰:「持其志, 無暴其氣」。(*Mengzi* 3.2/15/20)

By contrast, the *xing* 形 – literally form or shape – is visible, with clear boundaries, and refers to the body's outline. It has nothing to do with a person as a whole; it is not conscious and has no personality or sense of self. There are important differences between frames and forms. Body frames involve relationships between wholes and parts; body forms involve relationships between inner and outer (Sommer 2008, which provides a detailed account of differences between *ti*, *xing*, and *shēn*).

Shēn refers to a body, person, or "embodied person," both as a lived physical body and as a socially constructed personality. As lived in bodies, *shēn* can be measured in space (height) and time (lifespan). The physical boundaries of one *shēn* do not overlap those of another. As social constructions, *shēn* have characteristics such as status, personal identity, character, moral values, and experience. *Shēn* are self-aware and are the locus of inner reflection and self-cultivation. They are materially discrete, but socially permeable, and can absorb social attributes such as honor, disgrace, and so on (Sommer 2008).

Finally, the term *ren* 人 or "person" refers to the entire person, including the *shēn*, heart-mind, and spirit (Ames 1993).

1.3.2 The Heart-Mind

Most texts attribute consciousness and thought to the *xin*, a term that refers to the mind but also to the heart, located in the center of the chest (Y. Lo 2003). This term is especially difficult to translate, and there is no consensus whether to call it "mind" or "heart"; I use the perhaps awkward "heart-mind." Several psychological attributes are associated with the heart-mind: will or intentions (*zhi* 志), knowledge or consciousness (*zhi* 知), desires (*yu* 欲), and thought or awareness (*yi* 意).

There are important differences between Chinese and Western understandings of heart and mind, and the cognitive linguist Ning Yu has argued that Chinese cultural conceptualizations of the heart or mind differ fundamentally from Western dualism, because the "heart" (*xin*) is understood as the central faculty of both affective and cognitive activity and also as the source of thought, feelings, and emotions. By contrast, modern Western philosophy asserts a dichotomy between reason and emotion in which thoughts and ideas are linked to a largely disembodied "mind" and desires and emotions with an embodied "heart" (N. Yu 2007: 27–28, cf. Damasio 1994, Lakoff and Johnson 1999). By contrast, early Chinese philosophy understood "heart" and "mind" as one *xin* 心: "the core of affective and cognitive structure, conceived of as having the capacity for logical reasoning, rational understanding, moral will, intuitive imagination, and aesthetic feeling, unifying human will, desire, emotion, intuition, reason and thought" (N. Yu 2007: 28).

In mind-centered texts especially, the heart-mind was importantly considered the ruler of the body or the senses. In a major study of the body as an organization of space in early China, Mark Edward Lewis identifies two contrasting metaphors of the body as state. In "harmonious" body-state metaphors, the mind rules the state, and the body or senses are functionaries within it. By contrast, in "agonistic" metaphors, body components – including the senses and emotions – contest the heart-mind's rulership (Lewis 2006: 37–39). These two metaphors provide two very different accounts of the heart-mind. The *Huangdi neijing* uses harmonious metaphors; here, the heart-mind is one of five yin "viscera" (*zang* 藏), and psychological functions are distributed harmoniously among the five. (The other four yin organs are the kidneys, liver, lungs, and spleen.) In the more prevalent agonistic metaphors, the mind asserts domination over the five sense organs – described as ministers or officials – who try to assert independence, and reject hierarchical control. This view appears in a wide range of Warring States and Western Han texts, including the *Guanzi*, *Mengzi*, and *Xunzi*. A potentially agonistic version of the metaphor appears in the text *Wuxing* 五行 (*Five Kinds of Action*), excavated from tombs at Mawangdui and Guodian. Here, the heart-mind rules the body as a ruler rules a state, and the senses are its servants or slaves.

A very different picture of the *xin* as heart appears in medical and recipe texts, which seem to have had different audiences and objectives than philosophical texts. Most describe *xin* straightforwardly as the heart, an organ in the center of the chest. For example, medical texts excavated from Mawangdui, Zhangjiashan

張家山 (Jingzhou, Hubei, 196–186 BCE), and Wuwei 武威 (Gansu, 25–220 CE) focus on description of ailments associated with the heart (*xin*) and spirit and accounts of therapies that involve them.

These medical passages treat *xin* in relative isolation, in contexts that are clearly diagnostic or therapeutic. Within these contexts, the absence of cosmological analogies or other theoretical content is not surprising. As in the multi-authored Greek Hippocratic corpus, treatises range considerably in content and audience from the clearly medical to the rhetorical, philosophical, and cosmological.

1.3.3 Spirits

Several terms with complex semantic fields refer to spirit or "soul" (*shén* 神). In its oldest uses, *shén* referred to extra- (or formerly) human entities, including ancestors, divine powers, and the inhabitants of mountains, lakes, and forests. These powers needed to be identified and placated. The term also came to be used of human beings of extraordinary sagacity who become "like" spirits. The term is also used of a "spirit" quality within humans that makes them "spirit-like." In some medical contexts, spirit is one of the fundamental and necessary constituents of a living human being.

References to external, extra-human spirits begin with the oracle bone inscriptions. They appear repeatedly in the *Book of Odes* and *Book of Rites*, and, less frequently, in the Confucian *Analects*. Ritual texts – the *Liji* especially – address the role of sacrifice and other methods to achieve the presence of extra-human spirits. In Masters texts, discussions of spirit are divided between debates about the nature of extra-human *shén*, how humans should relate to them, and the nature and limits of their consciousness.

Starting in the fourth century, the view arose that individuals could store, enhance, and refine spirit internally. This internal spirit was closely linked to essence (*jing*) and *qi*. Importantly, it was independent of ritual relations with external spirits. Accounts of internal spirit are prominent in the *Guanzi*, *Zhuangzi*, and Xunzi, as well as in excavated texts from Mawangdui and Guodian. It is also prominent in medical texts as an important component of a person, which must be preserved and kept from harm. According to Puett, the term *spirit* was only applied to intra-human refined *qi* in the Warring States period, when the term's meaning was redefined by ongoing debates about the nature of both spirits and spirit powers (Puett 2002: 21–23). Advocates of new self-cultivation practices claimed that self-cultivation practices could offer spirit-like powers to humans, and thus tried to reduce the difference between spirits and humans.

Another meaning of *shén*, primarily in a medical context, is the animating force that maintains life in a living body. Living bodies are vivified by essence (*jing*), *qi*, and spirit, and when spirit leaves the body, it dies. For example, in the *Huainanzi*:

> The form is the residence of life; *qi* is the origin of life; spirit is the governor of life. If [even] one loses its place, then [all] three are harmed.
>
> 夫形者, 生之所也; 氣者, 生之元也; 神者, 生之制也。一失位, 則三者傷矣. *Huainanzi* 1/9/15–16, *Yuandao* 原道)

2 Mind-Centered Texts

The mind-centered view has two separable components. One is claims for the hegemony of the mind over the body or the senses. The other is claims for correspondence or alliance between the heart-mind (*xin*) and internal spirit (*shén*), hand in hand with arguments for the importance of spirit. Mind-centered texts tend to recommend using self-cultivation procedures to enhance internal spirit within the body. They also identify internal spirit with virtue and with the heart-mind; and describe the heart-mind and spirit ruling the body as ruler rules the people or a state. They thus present a binary view of a person as a polarity between the body and the mind/spirit. These views developed over time, including the incorporation of spirit into the capabilities of the mind-ruler. This view is most prominent in the *Analects*, *Mengzi*, and *Xunzi*; and also appears in a range of texts that make body-state microcosm-macrocosm analogies, including some sections of the *Guanzi* and the *Huangdi neijing*. Although they fall short of a strict definition of mind-body or mind/spirit-body dualism, these mind-centered descriptions, including heart-mind as ruler metaphors, repeatedly draw contrasts between the body and mind and spirit.

2.1 The *Analects* And *Mozi*

The *Analects* of Confucius forms the backdrop for later views. It offers two interrelated views of the body. On the one hand, it stresses the importance of correct alignment for both ethical and political virtue. It also describes the correct alignment of the body as a key element of ritual conduct and a central element of the efficacy of ritual. The *Analects* has much to say about the body, the *shēn* person especially, but relatively little to say about mind or spirit. It combines a strong interest in ritual – for human purposes – with respectful distance from spirits, understood as external spirits rather than to human psychological capacities.

Confucius repeatedly describes ritual as a powerful technique for aligning the body correctly, and for aligning body and mind. For Confucius, ritual is inherently embodied, and would be incomprehensible otherwise. The *Liji* records a remark attributed to Confucius about things that don't exist":

> Soundless music, disembodied ritual, and mourning without [mourning] clothes— these are what is called the three things that don't exist.
>
> 無聲之樂, 無體之禮, 無服之喪, 此之謂三無 (*Liji* 30.2/138/10–11)

The *Analects* emphasizes the need for correct physical disposition of the *shēn* body as the basis for virtue and efficacious action. *Analects* 13.6 remarks:

> If the person is correctly aligned, then there will be obedience without orders being given. If it is not correct, there will not be obedience even though orders are given.
>
> 其身正, 不令而行; 其身不正, 雖令不從 (*Lunyu* 13.6/34/13)[6]

But what does it mean to be "aligned"? The term *zheng* is often translated as upright or "right" in the normative sense of being morally upright. But it can also refer to the correct alignment of physical objects. For example, in the *Analects*, *zheng* can also refer to aligning an object, including one's own body. Thus, a "gentleman" or an exemplary person (*junzi* 君子) maintains a dignified appearance by straightening – which is to say, aligning – his robe and cap (20.2). He does not sit if his mat is not aligned correctly (*buzheng* 不正, 10.9), and aligns his mat before accepting a gift of meat (10.13). He is advised (8.4) to *zheng yanse* 正顏色 – literally to rectify his facial coloring – in order to encourage sincerity and trustworthiness in others. Finally, gentlemen associate with others who follow *dao* in order to be set right by them (1.14).

The notion of correct alignment also applies to government, for example, at 12.17: "To govern (*zheng* 政) means to align (*zheng* 正). If you set an example by [your own] alignment, who will dare not to be aligned?" (*Lunyu* 12.17/32/18). Finally, the sage-ruler Shun is described as governing, simply by aligning himself correctly to face south:

> As for one who ruled by means of *wuwei* was it not Shun? How did he do it? He made himself reverent and aligned himself [in the ritually correct way] facing south, and that was all.
>
> 無為而治者, 其舜也與? 夫何為哉, 恭己正南面而已矣 (*Lunyu* 15.5/42/9)

---

[6] Translations of the *Analects* are my own, but I have consulted Lau 1992 and Slingerland 2003a.

These examples show how much importance Confucius attached to the body. Confucius repeatedly describes ritual as a powerful technique for aligning the body correctly and for aligning body and mind. (There are also close philological links between the terms for ritual (*li* 禮) and the *ti* 體 body.)

The *Analects* also underscores the importance of the body to virtuous conduct and ritual by the relative absence of accounts of the heart-mind. The term *xin* occurs only five times, and without reference to either bodies or spirits. Confucius speaks of his own *xin* in a famous account of his own development:

> At fifteen, I set my will on learning. At thirty, I took my place. At forty, I had no doubts. At fifty, I understood the mandate of Heaven. At sixty, my ear was compliant. At seventy, I could follow the desires of my heart-mind (*xin suo yu* 心所欲) without going beyond the rule [the carpenter's square]. (*Lunyu* 2.4/3/1–2)

His remark links the heart-mind to desires. Another passage links the heart-mind to virtue, describing Yan Hui as capable of spending three months with "nothing in his heart-mind but humaneness" (6.7/12/19).

References to *shén* in the *Analects* clearly denote external spirits, rather than human psychological capacities. Confucius is famously reticent about spirits, and "does not discuss prodigies, feats of strength, disorderly chaos or spirits" (7.21). He goes further and defines the virtue of wisdom as an attitude in which one "respects spirits but keeps them at a distance" (6.22). These remarks are clear that humans should not engage with spirit powers or try to influence them. As Puett puts it, the purpose of ritual should be not to influence spirits but to cultivate ourselves. We should revere spirits, but the best way to revere them is not to try to influence them (Puett 2002: 98).

In summary, the *Analects* has much to say about the embodied person, but little to say about the heart-mind and either spirits or spirit capacities. He combines a strong interest in ritual – for human purposes – with respectful distance from spirits.

Early and late Mohist treatments of body, mind, and spirit differ considerably. Early Mohist texts discuss spirits at length; by contrast, the epistemological chapters engage in definitions of key terms.[7]

In strong contrast to the *Analects*, the term *xin* occurs over fifty times in the *Mozi*. Sometimes, it refers to affective states, such "not having a peaceful heart-mind" (*wu an xin* 無安心, 1.1/1/10) or "having no remorse in one's heart-mind" (*wu yuan xin* 無怨心, 1.1/1/12). Other passages use the term *xin* to refer to a cognitive faculty, often attributed to a superior person or *junzi*. For example,

---

[7] The *Mozi*, associated with Mo Di 墨翟 (fl. c.430 BCE) consists of seventy-one chapters, in six groups, of which eighteen are no longer extant. See Graham 1985 and Fraser 2016 and 2020.

superior persons ensure that destructive thoughts and impulses are not present in their heart-minds (*wu cun zhi xin* 無存之心, *Mozi* 1.2/2/14, ch. 2). The same chapter links a superior person's wisdom to a mental faculty of discrimination: "For those who are intelligent, their heart-minds make distinctions" (*hui zhe xin bian* 慧者心辯, *Mozi* 1.2/3/2, ch. 2). Thus, although the heart-mind can be an affective faculty that feels peace, grief, etc., the *Mozi* also describes the heart-mind as an explicitly cognitive faculty that discriminates and thinks.

The early Mohist chapters include extensive discussion of external spirits and postmortem consciousness in accounts of "ghosts and spirits" (*guishen* 鬼神). These discussions focused on three issues concerning ghosts and spirits: whether they existed, whether they had consciousness (*ming* 明), and extended critiques of Ru attitudes and practices toward them. Three chapters titled "Explaining Ghosts" (*Minggui* 明鬼, 29–31) present examples of interactions between humans and spirits, and demonstrated human shortcomings.[8] The early Mohists believed that spirits were conscious, had foreknowledge of human actions, and could reward the worthy and punish the unworthy. These beliefs helped promote order in the world:

> Now, if we could persuade the people under Heaven to believe that ghosts and spirits are capable of rewarding the worthy and punishing the wicked, then how could there ever be disorder in the world?
>
> 偕若信鬼神之能賞賢而罰暴也，則夫天下豈亂哉！(*Mozi* 8.3/50/26–27, ch. 31, Sterckx 2007: 28)

Several definitions in the Mohist epistemological chapters describe how bodies and minds were constituted. The dialectical chapters define *ti* as limbs or "parts" in contrast to wholes. They define life as holding together the intelligence and physical form.[9] Here, intelligence and physical form are distinct entities that share a location in space, and both are prerequisites for life in a human being.

The text does not explore the logical implications of this coexistence in physical space, nor does it address the question of what happens to the body-intelligence composite after death, when the intelligence is no longer bound to the physical form. Finally, the passage identifies life as the coexistence, suggesting that the mind cannot survive the body, and the body requires the heart-mind to be alive.

---

[8] See Sterckx 2007: 26–30. Additional accounts of the perspicacity of ghosts and spirits come from the Shanghai Museum excavated Chu manuscript "The Perspicuity of Ghosts and Spirits" (*Guishén zhi ming* 鬼神之明). See Ma Chengyuan 2005 (*Shanghai bowuguan* vol. 5): 307–321. For discussion see Brindley 2009 and Ding 2006 and 2011.

[9] 生，形與知處也. *Mozi* 10.1.43/69/25, ch. 43, cf. Graham 1978: 280.

2.2 The *Mengzi*

The mind-centered view first becomes prominent in the *Mengzi* (also known as the *Mencius*). It emphasizes the importance of the heart-mind – including its role as the ruler of the body and senses – and considers spirit as a capacity beyond even sagacity. These two views inform Mencian understandings of the body.

Mencius repeatedly refers to the heart-mind. He links it to virtue in his account of the four "sprouts" of virtue and considers it the "greatest" part of a person. It is also central to his account of self-cultivation by the refinement of *qi*. At 2A2 Mengzi claims to have attained an "unperturbed mind" (*budongxin* 不動心) at the age of forty; and describes *qi* as filling the frame of the body, commanded by the will: "The will is the commander of the *qi*; *qi* is what fills the frame."[10]

Mengzi goes on to describe the body as a container: filled by "flood-like *qi*" and containing the heart-mind. The container is permeable: *qi* can enter the body and emanate from it without loss. An aspect of that permeability is the body's "transparency." When a person is "upright within the breast" (*xiong zhong zheng* 胸中正), the pupils of the eye are clear and bright (4A15). The virtue of exemplary persons manifests in their limbs and coloring (7A21).

Unlike the *Guanzi*, which links *qi* with essence and spirit (discussed in Section 3.1), Mengzi does not discuss essence (*jing*). Mengzi describes the body as filled with flood-like *qi* and containing the heart-mind. Mengzi also describes the body as transparent in the sense that the state of the heart-mind is visible in the appearance of the body. If a person is internally upright, the pupils of the eye are clear and bright (4A15, 7.15/38/14–15). According to 7A21, an exemplary person's true nature – humaneness, rightness, the rites and wisdom – is rooted in the heart-mind but manifests in his coloration by giving the face a sleek appearance and is also visible in the back and limbs (*Mengzi* 13.21/69/14–15).

2.2.1 The Heart-Mind in Mencian Moral Psychology

Having an unmoved heart-mind is important for Mengzi because it manages the will and through it, the *qi*. But the unmoved heart-mind only nourishes floodlike *qi* if it itself is nourished with rightness and propriety (*yi* 義). According to Kwong-loi Shun, the heart-mind can only be unmoved if the will – which governs the *qi* – accords with rightness and propriety. Cultivating *qi* is thus

---
[10] 夫志、氣之帥也,氣、體之充也. *Mengzi* 3.2/15/20. Translations are indebted to Lau 1984 and Gassmann 2011.

necessary to support the will. The unmoved heart-mind is what makes the will conform to rightness and propriety (Shun 1997: 75–76, 84). Mengzi's innovation here is to link *qi* cultivation to moral excellence. As Alan Chan puts it, for Mengzi, "floodlike *qi*" is the moral vigor of a sage; *qi* thus shapes the heart-mind, and this fundamental insight underlies Mengzi's approach to ethical life. Chan (like Shun) takes the will as the aim or direction of the heart-mind, and necessary to set the heart-mind in a firm direction. However, well-nourished *qi* is not sufficient to direct the heart-mind, since it can also be set in a wrong direction (A. Chan 2002: 43 and 47).

Mengzi's claim that *qi* fills the body was conventional by this time, but his claim that the heart-mind commands it (via the will) is more complex. It is not clear whether Mengzi thinks that *qi* always follows the dictates of the heart-mind because *qi* is controlled by the will, rather than the heart-mind. The problem is that everything we do affects our *qi*. Thus, the heart-mind could only command the *qi* if it could control its affective and cognitive movements, especially likes and dislikes. The *Zuozhuan*, Gaozi, and *Mengzi* (and also the *Zhuangzi* and the Guodian texts) agree on the importance of regulating the will, so that it does not succumb to the excesses of *qi*. What distinguishes Mengzi's approach to self-cultivation is his focus on the importance of the heart-mind's control of the *qi*, and how to achieve it.

At issue is how the heart-mind is directed. Chan suggests that Mengzi's important innovation is the view that we can nourish qi so that the resulting "floodlike *qi*" becomes one with rightness and propriety. But this can only happen if the qi is consistently nourished by rightness and propriety, since our tastes and preferences affect the qi. Here Mengzi disagrees with Gaozi, who relies on learning from external sources. Mencius takes the source of rightness and propriety to be internal. According to Chan, the heart-mind has an inherent inclination toward rightness and propriety, so that feelings of commiseration and respect arise naturally (A. Chan 2002).

This point is pursued in 2A6, where Mencius famously argues that all persons have a heart-mind that cannot endure the sufferings of others (*buren ren zhi xin* 不忍人之心). This "mind" is the basis of the four sprouts of virtue (3.6/ 18/ 4). He identifies four innate "heart-minds" that are inherent in human nature:

> Anyone without a mind for empathy and compassion is not human; anyone without a mind for shame and repulsion is not human; anyone without a mind for politeness and respect is not human; and anyone without a mind for right and wrong is not human.

無惻隱之心, 非人也; 無羞惡之心, 非人也; 無辭讓之心, 非人也; 無是非之心, 非人也. (*Mengzi* 3.6/18/7–8)[11]

He considers these four tendencies to be the origin of four major virtues and identifies each tendency as a "mind." The mind that feels empathy and compassion is the "sprout" (*duan* 端) of the virtue of humaneness (*ren* 仁); the mind that feels shame and dislike is the sprout of rightness and propriety (*yi*). The mind that feels modesty and courtesy is the sprout of ritual propriety (*li* 禮), and the mind that distinguishes right from wrong is the sprout of wisdom (*zhi* 智). These four tendencies are as inherent in our nature as having four limbs (*Mengzi* 3.6/18/8–9). These tendencies resist classification as either purely "affective" or "rational"; the result is a distinctive Mencian conception of practical reason (D. Wong 1991, Shun 1997). Mengzi thus redefines the mind as a central part of ethical life.

It is in this context that he briefly mentions the heart-mind's relation to the senses. At 6A15 he argues that individual morality depends on which part of a person guides and controls. That is, whether one follows the greater or more petty part of oneself. Here, the senses play a role. He argues that "the offices of the eyes and ears cannot think, and can be confused by things; it is the office of the heart-mind that can think.[12] He thus uses the relation of the heart-mind to the senses to account for ethical failure, which occurs when people follow their less important part (the senses) instead of their greater part (the heart-mind). Mengzi thus locates ethical failure in the senses but stops short of claiming the heart-mind's rule over the senses (Shun 1997: 175–77). The full version of that claim is put forward by Xunzi.

2.2.2 Mengzi on Spirit

Mengzi has little to say about spirit; the term *shén* appears only three times in the *Mengzi*. One is a clear reference to external spirits, and two passages discuss internal *shén*. At 7A.13 he remarks that an exemplary person (*junzi*) manifests spirit. The context is a contrast between the influence of a gentleman, a hegemon (*ba* 霸), and a true king (*wang* 王). A hegemon makes the people happy; a true king makes them deeply content, but where a gentlemen passes, transformation occurs and where he resides is spirit-like.[13] This influence surpasses even that of a true king.

At 7B25, spirit is at the apex of a moral hierarchy:

> What is appropriate to desire is called good; but to have it in oneself is called trustworthy. To be filled with it and instantiate it is called beautiful; but to be filled with it, instantiate it, and shine it forth is called great. To be great and

---

[11] Translations of the *Mengzi* are indebted to Gassmann 2011 and Lau 1984.
[12] 耳目之官不思, 而蔽於物 ... 心之官則思 *Mengzi* 11.15/60/27–28.
[13] 夫君子所過者化, 所存者神. *Mengzi* 13.13/68/19–21.

thus transform others is called being a sage; but to be a sage whose sagacity is is impossible to understand is called "spirit."

可欲之謂善，有諸己之謂信，充實之謂美，充實而有光輝之謂大，大而化之之謂聖，聖而不可知之之謂神。(*Mengzi* 14.25/76/4)

In this hierarchy of excellences, when sagacity reaches a level that is impossible to understand, it is called *shén*. These passages clearly portray spirit as an internal quality, even sagehood. Mengzi suggests the mind's rule over the senses, but he does not elaborate, nor does he link spirit to claims for the mind's rulership of the body. These steps are taken by Xunzi.

2.3 Xunzi

Mengzi gave a new importance to the mind by taking its affective and cognitive capacities as the origin of moral development. Xunzi goes several steps farther. First he makes the explicit claim that the mind is the ruler of the body and the senses. Second, he explicitly identifies it as the source of thinking and evaluative judgments, including the assessment of feelings. Third, he explicitly links the activity of the mind to spirit. Xunzi explicitly posits the heart-mind as the ruler of the body and the senses, which function as the heart-mind's ministers:

> When the work of Heaven has been established and the accomplishments of Heaven have been completed, the form is set and spirit arises. Liking, dislikes, happiness, anger, sorrow, and joy are contained therein – these are called one's Heavenly Dispositions. The eyes, ears, nose, and mouth each has its own form and its respective objects and they cannot assume each others' abilities – these are called one's Heavenly Officials. The heart-mind inhabits the central cavity so as to govern the Five Officials; for this reason it is called one's Heavenly Lord.
>
> 天職既立，天功既成，形具而神生，好惡喜怒哀樂臧焉，夫是之謂天情。耳目鼻口形能各有接而不相能也，夫是之謂天官。心居中虛，以治五官，夫是之謂天君 (*Xunzi* 17/80/9–10).[14]

Here the heart-mind inhabits its central cavity of the body, just as a ruler governs from the center of a state. This container is semi-porous. Information moves from the outside in; orders and instructions issue from the inside out.

2.3.1 Xin *And Cognition*

Xunzi considers the heart-mind the source of cognition and moral judgments; the heart-mind is the faculty that can understand *dao*, which allows it to make

---

[14] Translations are indebted to Hutton 2014 and Knoblock 1988–1994.

correct judgments. He attributes this faculty to the qualities of emptiness (*xu* 虛), unity (*yi* 壹), and stillness (*jing* 靜): "How do people know *dao*? I say: with the heart-mind. How does the heart-mind know? I say: it is through emptiness, unity, and stillness."[15] He goes on to explain: "People are born and have awareness; with awareness they have intention."[16] People are born with awareness because "The heart-mind is born and has awareness. With understanding comes awareness of differences."[17] He explains that the heart-mind has emptiness even though having intentions means that it is always storing something. It has unity even though it is aware of differences. The heart-mind is always in motion, but – if properly cultivated – it maintains stillness by not letting its movements disorder its understanding.

He uses the metaphor of a mirror created by still water to describe this stillness: "Hence, the human heart-mind may be compared to a pan of water."[18] If you keep it upright and still, the mud sinks to the bottom, and the water is clear enough to see your face in detail. But even the slightest movement stirs the mud and muddles the water's clarity. "The heart-mind is just like this" (*xin yi ru shi yi* 心亦如是矣, *Xunzi* 21/104/8).

Xunzi describes the heart-mind as making cognitive judgments based on the inputs of the senses and the body: it uses the inputs of the different senses to differentiate different kinds of things. Xunzi emphasizes that these distinctions should be reflected by correct names. The passage begins with the different kinds of information that are differentiated (*yi* 異) by the individual senses and the body overall:

> Form and structure, color, and pattern (*xing ti, se li* 形體, 色理) are differentiated (*yi* 異) by means of the eyes. Notes, tones, clear highs, muddy lows, mode, measure and strange sounds are differentiated by means of the ears. Sweet, bitter, salty, bland, piquant, sour, and other strange flavors are differentiated by the mouth. Fragrant, foul, flowery, rotten, putrid, sharp, sour, and other strange smells are differentiated by the nose. Pain, itch, cold, hot, slippery, sharp, light, and heavy are differentiated by the form and frame (*xingti* 形體). Persuasions, reasons, happiness, anger, sorrow, joy, love, hate, and desire are differentiated by the heart-mind (*Xunzi* 22/108/16–109/1).[19]

Each corporeal faculty thus engages in its own proper area of discrimination and differentiates its proper sensory input. At the end of the sequence is the heart-mind, which differentiates emotions, desires, and reason.

---

[15] 人何以知道? 曰: 心。心何以知? 曰: 虛壹而靜. *Xunzi* 21/103/22.
[16] 人生而有知, 知而有志. *Xunzi* 21/104/1.   [17] 心生而有知, 知而有異. *Xunzi* 21/104/2.
[18] 故人心譬如槃水. *Xunzi* 21/104/7.
[19] For musical technical terms see Knoblock 1994, 3: 336.26.

In addition, the heart-mind seems to have a unique power to judge its own awareness (though the meaning of this line is unclear, and any reading is necessarily interpretive): "The heart-mind has the power to judge its awareness" (*xin you zhi zhi* 心有徵知. *Xunzi* 22/109/1). Once it judges its awareness, it can understand the sounds and forms made available by the ears and eyes. But it can only do so after sensory faculties encounter their objects:

> Judging awareness must await the Heaven-given faculties (*tian guan* 天官) to appropriately encounter their respective kinds and only then can it work. If the five faculties (*wu guan* 五官) encounter them but have no awareness (*zhi* 知), or if the heart-mind judges among them but has no persuasive explanations (*shuo* 說) [for its judgments], then everyone will say that such a person does not know. (*Xunzi* 22/109/2–3)

Only after this process is complete is it possible to name things (*Xunzi* 22/109/5). Xunzi's moral psychology is distinctive for this new emphasis on cognition, understood as the critical and reflective understanding of the heart-mind.

Xunzi also emphasizes that, although the ability to think is a natural human aptitude, this kind of reflective thinking is not natural, and is the product of deliberate effort, which he describes as "deliberate artifice" (*wei* 偽):

> The feelings of liking, disliking, happiness, anger, sadness and joy in one's nature are called dispositions (*qing* 情). When there is a certain disposition and the heart-mind makes a choice on its behalf, this is called reflection (*lü* 慮). When the heart-mind reflects and the abilities act on it, this is called deliberate artifice (*wei* 偽). That which comes into being through accumulated reflection and training of one's abilities is also called deliberate artifice. (*Xunzi* 22/107/23–24)[20]

In summary, Xunzi attributes to the heart-mind a new and unique autonomy to govern, including the ability to accept what it thinks right, choose among emotions, and approve and disapprove of desires.[21] He thus presents the heart-mind as the faculty that rules the body, engages in cognition and reflection, and apprehends *dao*: "What the heart-mind deems to be right it accepts; what it deems wrong it rejects."[22] In his view, "order and disorder reside in what the heart-mind approves of, they are not present in the desires from one's dispositions."[23]

---

[20] On this point see Lee 2005: 42.
[21] By "autonomy" in relationship to the heart-mind I mean its independence from the rest of the body and the emotions especially. This context is very different than Henry Rosemont and Roger Ames' use of the term in their critiques of "autonomous" right-bearing individuals as distinct from Confucian role-bearing individuals (Rosemont and Ames 2016).
[22] 是之則受, 非之則辭. *Xunzi* 21/104/12.
[23] 故治亂在於心之所可, 亡於情之所欲. *Xunzi* 22/111/11.

This description goes well beyond the *Mengzi*. Xunzi defines the heart-mind in a new way by making it the active agent of self-cultivation. It is the site of all psychological phenomena, including sensation, emotion, and desires. But for the heart-mind to engage in critical thinking, it must have a volitional power that allows it to be independent of desires and emotions. The heart-mind's autonomy is what allows it to supervise the senses, emotions, and desires; its faculty of appropriateness is what allows it to engage in deliberate effort. On this view, human morality has a tenuous connection with Heaven, but a very close connection to the activity of the heart-mind (Lee 2005: 37–40).

2.3.2 Xunzi on Mind And Spirit

Xunzi's third innovation is explicitly linking the heart-mind to internal spirit. Like Mengzi, he takes a pragmatic view of external spirit(s), which he understands as how the cosmos operates as it does: "We cannot see the activity, but we can see the accomplishments. This is what we call spirit."[24] But Xunzi is also explicit that humans have internal spirit. For example, he describes what he calls methods to control *qi* and nourish the heart-mind in order to become "spirit-like": "In the arts of controlling *qi* and nourishing the heart-mind, nothing is more direct than following ritual, nothing is more important than getting a good teacher, and nothing is [more] spirit-like than single-minded liking [of these practices]."[25] Elsewhere, he recommends integrity (*cheng* 誠) as the way to cultivate the heart-mind (*yangxin* 養心) and achieve spirit powers: "If, with a heart-mind of integrity, you cling to humaneness (*ren*) you will embody it [integrity]; if you embody it, you will be a spirit; if you are a spirit, you will be able to transform things."[26] Spirit, however, is not inherently moral; some people are "knowing but dangerous, harmful but spirit-like, skilled at deceit but clever."[27]

Xunzi disagrees with Mengzi's view of spirit as a capacity that surpasses even sagehood. As Roel Sterckx puts it, Xunzi understands *shén* as a spirit-like power that can transform and harmonize the world through the activity of a ruler who governs without apparent effort. His understanding of *shén* is thus grounded in notions of order and hierarchy, both social and cosmic (Sterckx 2007: 27). The order that results from such a sage-ruler's activity is *shén*: "To achieve the utmost goodness and to uphold proper order is called being spirit[- like]. To be so that none of the ten thousand things can overturn you is called being firm. One who is

---

[24] 不見其事而見其功, 夫是之謂神. *Xunzi* 17/80/6. On this point see Puett 2002: 185–88.
[25] 凡治氣養心之術, 莫徑由禮, 莫要得師, 莫神一好. *Xunzi* 2/6/9–10.
[26] 誠心守仁則形, 形則神, 神則能化矣. *Xunzi* 3/11/4.
[27] 知而險, 賊而神, 為詐而巧. *Xunzi* 6/23/7.

spirit[- like] and firm is called a sage."²⁸ In other words, spirit can be used to transform the people. If an enlightened lord uses power and *dao* to control the people, their transformation by *dao* is spirit-like" (*ruo shén* 如神, 8/31/5).

Xunzi also describes spirit illumination (*shénmíng* 神明) as a property of the heart-mind. He considers the heart-mind to be both the ruler of the body and the master of *shénmíng*:

> The heart-mind is the lord of the form (*xing zhi jun* 形之君) and the master of *shénmíng* (*shénmíng zhi zhu* 神明之主). It issues orders, but it takes orders from nothing ... thus, the mouth can be compelled either to be silent or to speak, and the body can be compelled, either to contract or to extend itself, but the heart-mind cannot be compelled to change its thoughts. What it considers right, one accepts, what it consider wrong, one rejects. (*Xunzi* 21/ 104/10–12)

Xunzi thus links the heart-mind's control over the body to its mastery of spirit illumination; he thus assimilates spirit-like powers to the normative activity of the heart-mind.

Texts excavated from Guodian present views very similar to those of Xunzi, with several accounts of relations between body and mind.²⁹ Two texts argue that the mind rules the body as a ruler rules a state. According to *Five Kinds of Action (Wuxing* 五行): "The ears, eyes, nose, mouth, hands, and feet – these six are the slaves of the mind."³⁰ Another Guodian text, "Black Robes" (*Ziyi*), presents a very different metaphor: "The people take the ruler as their mind; the ruler takes the people as his frame. When the mind is fond of something the frame is at peace with it; when the ruler is fond of something the people desire it."³¹ Here, authority arises from mutual recognition and assent between the ruler and the ruled. These two passages present entirely different metaphors of the mind as ruler. In one, the mind governs the body in agonistic relationship of master to servant; the other presents a harmonious relationship in which a ruler's authority comes from mutual recognition and consensus.

2.4 Conclusion

This section has surveyed claims for the hegemony of the heart-mind across several Warring States texts. They assert the importance of the heart-mind and

---

[28] 盡善挾 (洽)〔治〕之謂神。萬物莫足以傾之之謂固。神固之謂聖人. Xunzi 8/ 31/3–5.
[29] The Guodian Chu bamboo strip texts (*Guodian Chu jian* 郭店楚簡) were unearthed in 1993 in Tomb no. 1, Guodian, Jingmen, Hubei, and probably date to the late fourth century. For translation see Cook 2012. For the Guodian texts, see S. Chan 2019.
[30] 耳目鼻口手足六者，心之役也. *Wuxing,* strips 45–46. For "slaves" (lit. corvée labor) I follow Liu Zhao (2003), which also accords another version of this text excavated from Mawangdui. For further discussion of this metaphor see S. Chan 2009.
[31] 民以君為心，君以民為體，心好則體安之，君好則民欲之. *Ziyi,* strips 8–9.

attribute to it the capacity to make normative or cognitive distinctions. Such arguments first appear in the *Analects* and continue to appear in the *Mozi*, *Mengzi*, and *Xunzi*, but these texts make this claim in very different ways. The *Analects* and *Mengzi* focus on the "heart" in the heart-mind, its affective capacities, and its ability to guide desires. The *Mozi* and *Xunzi*, by contrast, call attention to its more narrowly cognitive capacities. (These capacities are in no way mutually exclusive, but are differences of emphasis.) Xunzi's views may well be indebted to the Mohists; they also resemble accounts of the centrality of the mind in several texts excavated from Guodian.[32]

A second claim is that the heart-mind is more important than, or has command over, the body or senses. Versions of this view appear in the *Mengzi*, *Xunzi*, in texts excavated from Guodian, and in the Tsinghua University bamboo slip texts. Some texts make the specific claim that the heart-mind *rules* the body or senses. This view appears in analogies between the mind's hegemony over the body and a ruler's hegemony over a state.

Finally, arguments about the role of spirit and its relation to the heart-mind appear in claims for correspondence or alliance between heart-mind and spirit. Xunzi in particular identified internal spirit with virtue and with the heart-mind. He thus aligns the heart-mind with spirit in a hierarchically superior relation to the body: the heart-mind and spirit rule the body as a ruler rules a state. The result is a binary view of a person in which the body is opposed to the mind or spirit.

3 Spirit-Centered Perspectives

I now turn to texts that both emphasize the importance of spirit and the body as sites of self-cultivation, and in some cases disparage or marginalize the activity of the mind. These texts all understand spirit (*shén*) as an internal faculty that is central to self-cultivation, and closely linked with *qi* and essence (*jing* 精), a product of refined *qi* that circulates in the body.[33] They all describe procedures whereby, if essence is sufficiently still (*jing* 靜) and unified (*yi* 一), it transforms into spirit and is stored in the heart-mind, and is the source of sagelike abilities. Spirit thus requires an adequate supply *qi* and essence. Such accounts occur in the "Inner Workings" (*Neiye* 內業) chapter of the *Guanzi*, the *Zhuangzi*, and

---

[32] Length constraints make it impossible to discuss important accounts of the mind in two other excavated texts. For the Guodian text "Human Nature Comes from the Mandate" (*Xingzi mingchu* 性自命出) see Perkins 2009 and Raphals 2019. For "The Heart-mind Is What Is Called the Center" (*Xin shi wei zhong* 心是謂中) from the Tsinghua University Warring States Bamboo Strips see Li Xueqin 2018. For a discussion and tentative translation see Raphals 2023: 112–114.

[33] Chiu 2016, cf. G. Chen 2006: 41–54, Graham 1989: 95–105, Roth 1990: 13–18.

several chapters of the *Huainanzi*. They share important similarities with the "Ten Questions" text from Mawangdui and with medical literature from approximately the first century BCE and later, starting with the *Huangdi neijing* (discussed in Section 4).

3.1 The *Guanzi*

Accounts of *shén* as an intrahuman capacity first appear in the *Guanzi*, a complex and composite text which presents polyvocal views of body, mind, and spirit. Accounts of persons as composites of body, mind, and spirit appear in two chapters titled "Arts of the Mind," 1 and 2 (*Xinshu shang, xia* 心術上, 下, chs. 36 and 37) and "Inner Workings" (*Neiye*, ch. 49). One difficulty is that text order does not indicate age. "Inner Workings" is considered the oldest of the three, but is numerically the last; and ideas in "Arts of the Mind, 2" seem to derive from it. "Arts of the Mind, 1," the first of the sequence, is a completely separate work. A fourth chapter, "The Pure Mind" (*Baixin* 白心, ch. 38), expands on concepts from both "Inner Workings" and "Arts of the Mind, 1."

3.1.1 Refining Qi and Essence

The "Arts of the Mind" chapters closely link the heart-mind to *jing* and *qi*. A passage in "Arts of the Mind, 1" describes a "house" that can become the dwelling of spirit illumination (*shénming*): "Clean your mansion, open its gates! Once you have eliminated partiality and are without speech, spirit illumination will appear."[34] An explanation of the passage, states that "mansion" refers to the mind and "gates" to the senses (specifically, the eyes and ears, *Guanzi* 13.1/96/16, ch. 36). The passage describes a deliberate emptying in order to allow the spontaneous entry of spirit illumination. This replacement is effected by the circulation of *jing* and leads to the practitioner becoming "enlightened (*ming* 明) and "spirit-like." Interestingly, the passage never mentions the mind: the heart-mind is simply a dwelling place that spirit enters and inhabits if the circumstances are correct.

Descriptions of body, mind, and spirit in terms of *jing* and *qi* continue in "Arts of the Mind, 2." It claims that "power" (*de* 德, a quasi-magical power or virtue, in the sense of "good at") will only come when the physical form is correctly aligned (*zheng* 正). But the heart-mind can only govern if body and heart-mind are quiescent (*jing* 靜). "Align the form and cultivate power; then all things may be fully grasped."[35]

---

[34] 潔其宮, 開其門, 去私毋言, 神明若存. *Guanzi* 13.1/96/7, ch. 36.
[35] 正形飾德, 萬物畢得. *Guanzi* 13.2/98/1, ch. 37.

Here the body and heart-mind work together to acquire powers associated with sages and the legendary rulers of antiquity. However, the passage turns to a potential conflict between a part of the body – the senses – and the heart-mind:

> Not to let things disorder the senses (*guan* 官) and not to let the senses disorder the heart-mind, this is called inner power (*nei de* 內德). And so, once thought and *qi* become stable (*yi qi ding* 意氣定), it [the form] becomes correctly aligned of itself (*ranhou you zheng* 然後反正). *Qi* is what fills the embodied person; in conduct, right alignment should be the guiding principle (*zheng zhi yi* 正之義). If what fills [the person] is not good, the heart-mind will not succeed. (*Guanzi* 13.2/98/1–3, ch. 37)

In this passage, the actions of the body (including sense perception) are distinguished from the actions of the mind, but they are not described as ontologically different. Rather they are a composite in which the mind does not rule the senses. The mind has normative functions – and a correctly ordered heart-mind affects the body – but inner power only comes when internal equilibrium prevents the senses disordering the heart-mind.

Because they are a composite, the state of the heart-mind is visible in the body. Correct alignment and quiescence are outwardly visible in firm muscles and sturdy bones. "A complete heart-mind within cannot be concealed. Outwardly it can be seen in the bearing, and it can be observed in the complexion."[36] This combination of correct alignment and quiescence strengthens muscle and bone, and also manifests in bearing (*xingrong* 形容) and coloration (*yanse* 顏色), emphasizing how pervasively body and mind affect each other. Here, self-cultivation depends not on textual study but on physical and possibly meditative practices.[37]

3.1.2 Spirit in "Inner Workings"

The view that *shén* is an intrahuman capacity is prominent in the *Guanzi* chapter "Inner Workings" (*Neiye*, ch. 49). It makes three claims about the development of spirit. First, essence (*jing*) is the basis of both physical life and sagacity; it is what constitutes both human internal spirit and external spirits are composed of the same stuff (essence). Second, essence can only lodge in a mind that is stable or settled (*dingxin*), and that cultivating the heart-mind (*xiuxin* 脩心) and making one's thoughts tranquil makes it possible to attain *dao*. However, third, the senses must be keen and the body must be strong (*Guanzi* 16.1/116/2–3, *ch.* 49). In other words, body and mind must cooperate to refine *qi* into essence.

---

[36] 金心在中不可匿。外見於形容, 可知於顏色. *Guanzi* 13.2/98/24–26, ch. 37.

[37] Mengzi makes similar claims in his account of cultivating "flood-like qi" (*haoran zhi qi* 浩然之氣, 2A2). Mark Csikszentmihalyi (2005) identifies this kind of argument with what he calls a "material virtue" tradition, also exemplified in the text "Five Kinds of Action" (*Wuxing* 五行), excavated from tombs at Guodian and Mawangdui.

The discussion of the heart-mind in "Arts of the Mind, 2" (Section 3.1.1, above) addressed the need for a "settled heart-mind" before *jing* and *qi* could be circulated and cultivated in the body. As the self-cultivation proceeds, attention shifts to the circulation of *jing* in the body and the entry of spirit. The *Neiye* begins by identifying essence (*jing*) as highly refined *qi* that is identified with life: "It is always the case that the essence of things is what makes them be alive."[38] *Jing* is also linked to both external spirits and the development of internal spirit and sagacity: "When it flows between Heaven and Earth, we call it ghosts and spirits; when it is stored within a person's chest, we call that person a sage.[39]

In other words, sages contain the same *jing* as external spirits (spirits are pure *jing*; humans are a mixture of *jing* and form), and *jing* is clearly identified with both spirit and sageliness. It is stored in the heart-mind, and eventually transformed into spirit. This can only happen if the heart-mind is settled:

> Only one who is capable of correct alignment and capable of stillness is, as a result, capable of being settled. When a settled heart-mind is present within, the ears and eyes are keen and bright, and the four limbs are durable and strong, is it possible to create a lodging place for essence. As for essence, it is the essence of *qi*. When *qi* is guided, it [essence] is generated.
>
> 能正能靜, 然后能定。定心在中, 耳目聰明, 四枝堅固, 可以為精舍。精也者, 氣之精者也。氣, 道乃生. (*Guanzi* 16.1/116/2–3, ch. 49)

The text then turns to spirit, understood as an internal faculty that can unify and transform. But the prerequisite for the entry of spirit illumination (*shénming* 神明) is the correct alignment of the body:

> If the form is not aligned, inner power will not come; if the center is not tranquil, the heart-mind will not be well ordered. Align the form, hold fast to inner power, and the extremity of spirit illumination will gradually arrive of itself.
>
> 形不正, 德不來; 中不靜, 心不治。正形攝德, 則淫然而自至神明之極 (*Guanzi* 16.1/116/11, ch. 49)

The passage concludes with a warning to not allow things to disorder the senses or to allow the senses to disorder the heart-mind.[40] The text then turns to spirit, which naturally resides in the body: "There is a spirit that of itself is present in the person, sometimes going, sometimes coming."[41] Its loss results in disorder,

---

[38] 凡物之精, (此) 〔比〕則為生. *Guanzi* 16.1/115/17, ch. 49.
[39] 流於天地之間, 謂之鬼神; 藏於胸中, 謂之聖人. *Guanzi* 16.1/115/18, ch. 49.
[40] 不以物亂官, 不以官亂心. *Guanzi* 16.1/116/12, ch. 49.
[41] 有神自在身, 一往一來. *Guanzi* 16.1/116/14, ch. 49.

and its presence ensures good order. If one carefully cleans its lodging place, essence comes of itself. This preparation involves the activity of the heart-mind:

> Refine your thoughts and contemplate it; make your thinking tranquil and put it in order. Be reverent, generous, dignified, and respectful, and essence will arrive and settle.
>
> 精想思之，寧念治之，嚴容畏敬，精將至定. (*Guanzi* 16.1/116/14–15, ch. 49)

These passages offer a picture of complex interactions between body, heart-mind, essence, and spirit. The process begins with aligning the body and settling the heart-mind: correct alignment of the body is a prerequisite for both an ordered heart-mind and spirit illumination. Spirit (*shén*) is described as naturally present within a person (*shēn*) and key to internal order. (The *Guanzi* never warns against "losing" one's mind, but repeatedly warns against losing spirit.)

The heart-mind is the lodging place of spirit, but also of a "mind within the mind" that seems to be linked with spirit:

> The mind thus stores the mind; within the mind there is another mind in it. In that mind within the mind, intention precedes words. Only after there is intention is there form; only after there is form are there words; only after words are there orders; only after orders is there order. If there is no order, disorder is inevitable. If there is disorder, there will be death.
>
> 心以藏心，心之中又有心焉。彼心之心，意以先言。 意然后形，形然后言。言然后使，使然后治。不治必亂，亂乃死 (*Guanzi* 16.1/116/21–22, ch. 49)

This "mind within the mind" seems to operate before sensory input; in contemporary terminology, it is precognitive. It is not explicitly identified with spirit.

The end of "Inner Workings" reiterates the importance of correct interactions between the body and heart-mind in order for spirit to arrive. First it is necessary to concentrate one's *qi* and align the body correctly: "Concentrate your *qi* like a spirit and the myriad things will all reside within."[42] It also reiterates the importance of the body:

> When the four limbs are aligned, and the blood and *qi* are stilled, unify your awareness, concentrate your heart-mind, and your ears and eyes will never go astray.
>
> 四體既正，血氣既靜，一意摶心，耳目不淫. (*Guanzi* 16.1/117/10, ch. 49)

---

[42] 摶氣如神，萬物備存. *Guanzi* 16.1/117/6, ch. 49.

The procedures described in the chapter start with aligning the body, which in turn aligns the heart-mind. The heart-mind in turn regulates the body and senses. The result is that spirit enters spontaneously, with powers normally ascribed to external spirits. This process clearly requires three elements – body, heart-mind, and spirit – that cannot be reduced to two. As a result, it does not fit dualist descriptions of body and mind (or body and spirit).

A difficulty in this account of spirit is how it arises in a person and why it is so important to retain and not deplete it. It clearly is not part of a person at birth, as it seems to be in the *Zhuangzi* and clearly is in the *Huainanzi* (discussed in Sections 3.2 and 3.3), and requires deliberate and sustained effort. Nor is it an "external" spirit or entity that is "invited" or that moves in from outside and can come and go at will. The distinction is that, after the preparations described in "Inner Workings," spirit arises internally, rather than coming in from the outside. At that point, this internal capacity or power becomes an important part of the person who has cultivated it, and depleting or losing spirit would cause the loss of the powers it entails.[43]

3.2 The *Zhuangzi*

The *Zhuangzi* is distinctive both for a negative view of the mind and a positive view of cultivating spirit, but with very different goals than those of the *Guanzi*.

3.2.1 Zhuangist Critiques of the Heart-Mind

The *Zhuangzi*'s attitude toward the heart-mind is complex. Several passages appear to belittle its activity, but other accounts of skills and practices clearly rely on it. The *Zhuangzi* appears to have two objections to the heart-mind. The first is to oppose the – by now – conventional view that it should be the ruler of the body.

A passage in the second chapter of the *Zhuangzi* seems to ridicule the view that the heart-mind should rule the body: "There seems to be a genuine commander, except we find no sign of it."[44] Which, the text asks, of the hundred bones, nine orifices, and six viscera present and complete in the body should we consider as closest to us? Do we have a favorite?

> If so, are the others all its servants? Are the servants unable to govern each other? Might they take turns being ruler and servant? Might there be a genuine ruler present among them?

---

[43] I am grateful to Erica Brindley for raising this question.
[44] 若有真宰, 而特不得其眹. *Zhuangzi* 2/4/1. Translations are based on Fraser 2024; I have also consulted Graham 1981 and Ziporyn 2020.

如是皆有為臣妾乎？其臣妾不足以相治乎？其遞相為君臣乎？其有真君存焉？ (*Zhuangzi* 2/4/2–4)

The text suggests that it is there is no inherent reason for the mind to rule and the rest of the body to be its servants, and asks, perhaps tongue-in-cheek, whether all the parts of the body should rule by turns.

The second objection is that the heart-mind actually obscures our ability to apprehend *dao*. In Chapter 4, a very Zhuangist Confucius instructs his student Yan Hui on a process of "fasting the heart-mind" (*zhai xin* 齋心):

> Listen not with your ears but with your heart-mind; listen not with your heart-mind but with your *qi*. Listening stops with the ears, the heart-mind stops with the tallies. The *qi* emptily waits on things. Only *dao* gathers emptiness. Emptiness is the fasting of the mind
>
> 无聽之以耳而聽之以心，无聽之以心而聽之以氣！聽止於耳，心止於符。氣也者，虛而待物者也。唯道集虛。虛者，心齋也 (*Zhuangzi* 4/10/1–3)

The phrase "the heart-mind stops with the tallies" indicates that what the mind grasps is the signs or symbols – the tallies – that it uses, but these tallies may not correspond well to actual circumstances. So the recommendation is to "listen," not with the heart-mind but with our actual constituent *qi*. Unlike the mind, it is "empty," open, and fluid (Fraser 2024: 255).

David B. Wong usefully explains this difference between attending the mind and attending the *qi* in terms of the difference between "top-down" and "bottom-up" thinking. The mind works by selecting and by making distinctions, both in empirical judgments that something is "so" or "not-so" (*shifei* 是非) but also that something is "right" or "wrong" (also *shifei*). Selection is necessary to get through the day, but it results in a partial and mediated access to the world. Contemporary theories of perception understand the mind to work both top-down and bottom-up. Perception is an interaction of bottom-up processes of receiving sensory input and top-down mental processes of both interpreting it and predicting future sensory inputs based on past assumptions and experience. But this process deprives us of much of our sensory input. The problem is that the perceptions and predictions of a "complete heart-mind" (*cheng xin* 成心) are insufficient to apprehend the varieties and divigations of *dao*. The text's point is that the more we attend – "listen" – to bottom-up sensation from the world, and the less we follow the top-down dictates of the mind, the better we will truly understand things. Seen in this way, "listening with the *qi*" suggests that it is possible to still the over-eager, top-down heart-mind and enhance the bottom-up processing of sensory information (probably through meditative practices). This approach to "listening with the *qi*" suggests the importance of the body not only in physical interaction with the world but in "thinking" (Wong 2024: 5–6).

Nonetheless, the heart-mind seems to be essential to many attitudes or practices the *Zhuangzi* praises or recommends. While the Zhuangist authors seem quite critical of the completed heart-mind, other passages refer more positively to a *xin* that is not fixed, and some of the skill masters (for example, the wheelwright Lun Bian) use their heart-minds in ways the Zhuangist authors endorse. These include the mastery of skill (discussed in Section 3.2.3) and the complex analytic activity that characterizes the arguments of several chapters, Chapter 2 especially.

3.2.2 Concentrating Spirit and the Body

In contrast to its ambivalent or critical view of the heart-mind, the *Zhuangzi* seems to view spirit in entirely positive terms. (The Zhuangist authors do not share the *Xunzi*'s warning that some people are "knowing but dangerous, harmful but spirit-like," discussed in Section 2.3.2.) The Zhuangist focuses on spirit in two contexts. One is accounts of the importance of "concentrating *shén*" and of spirit "dwelling within." The other is the use of spirit in the exercise of certain kinds of skill.

The *Zhuangzi* repeatedly presents the attitudes and behavior of a "spirit person" (*shénren* 神人) as different from – and superior to – the judgments and responses of the heart-mind. In Chapter 1 a "spirit person" makes grain ripen and protects animals from plagues by "concentrating *shén*" (*shén ning* 神凝, 1/2/16). Chapter 2 praises "realized persons" as "spirit-like"(*zhi ren shén yi* 至人神矣, *Zhuangzi* 2/6/17).

Other passages refer to spirit "inhabiting" the body in terms reminiscent of "Inner Workings." After its description of fasting the heart-mind (discussed in Section 3.2.1), Chapter 4 describes the entry of spirit as a consequence of pushing out the knowledge of the heart-mind:

> Let your ears and eyes connect within and push out the knowledge of the heart-mind, then ghosts and spirits will come and lodge [within].
>
> 夫徇耳目內通而外於心知, 鬼神將來舍. (*Zhuangzi* 4/10/7–8)

Several passages in Chapter 11 describe self-cultivation practices that nourish spirit by a – perhaps counter-intuitive – combination of aligning the body by withdrawing from sensation: "Don't look, don't listen; Enfold your spirit in stillness; The body will correct itself."[45] It continues:

---

[45] 无視无聽, 抱神以靜, 形將自正. *Zhuangzi* 11/27/24.

> "Let your eyes see nothing, your ears hear nothing, your heart-mind know nothing; Your spirit will guard your form and your form will live long.
>
> 目无所見, 耳无所聞, 心无所知, 女神將守形, 形乃長生. (*Zhuangzi* 11/27/25)

The passage concludes with the advice to "carefully guard your embodied person" (*shen shou nü shēn* 慎守女身 11/27/27). Another passage in the same chapter describes similar practices as "nourishing the heart-mind" (*xin yang* 心養):

> Simply abide in *wuwei*, and things will transform of themselves. Let the form and frame fall away; cast out hearing and vision . . . release your heart-mind and free your spirit.
>
> 汝徒處无為, 而物自化。墮爾形體, 吐爾聰明 . . . 解心釋神. (*Zhuangzi* 11/28/16–18)

These passages privilege spirit over the heart-mind, but also assert a strong relation to the body. On the one hand, they repeatedly urge putting the body or senses at a distance, but they also describe the body aligning itself correctly as a result.

3.2.3 Spirit and Skill

Chapter 3 and several passages in the Outer Chapters links spirit to the exercise of skill in depictions of hyper-aware individuals who excel at the performance of a craft or skill. In Chapter 3 the skilled butcher Pao Ding 庖丁 explains that he relies on spirit, rather than technical expertise in carving oxen:

> Now I meet it [the ox] with spirit rather than looking with my eyes. The knowledge of the senses stops, and then spirit urges proceed.
>
> 臣以神遇而不以目視, 官知止而神欲行. (*Zhuang*zi 3/8/5)

Pao Ding emphasizes that what he values is *dao*, not simple skill. As the scene concludes, the Lord Wenhui (whom he has been instructing) exclaims that Pao Ding's words have taught him how to nurture life (*yang sheng* 養生, *Zhuangzi* 3/8/11).

Chapter 19 describes several individuals of paramount skill, whose expertise requires a kind of concentrating that distances sensory input and focuses attention. A hunchback cicada catcher describes how he "empties his person" (*xu shēn* 處身) like a tree stump and holds out his arms like the branches of a withered tree; "for all the vastness of the world and the multitude of the myriad things, I am only aware of the cicada wings."⁴⁶ Although this is not a description of fasting the heart-mind, the cicada catcher uses the same technique for a different purpose. Similarly, when asked about his skill, the woodworker Zi Qing 梓慶 describes his preparations for making a bell stand as "fasting to still the heart-mind" (*zhai yi jing xin* 齊以靜心): "I forget that I have four limbs and a body."⁴⁷ He describes how "the skill concentrates" (*qi qiao zhuan* 其巧專) and outside distractions fade away (*wai gu xiao* 外骨消); only then does he go to the mountain forest to observe the inherent nature [of the trees]. "Only if there is [wood of] such perfect form that I completely see the bell stand in it, only then do I put my hand to it."⁴⁸ These passages do not use the term spirit, but nonetheless, these accounts all seem to describe a process of cultivating internal spirit by fasting or minimizing the influence of both the body and the heart-mind.

The last chapter of the *Zhuangzi* describes spirit as able to influence things outside the body. It describes realized individuals of antiquity as "complementing spirit illumination, nurturing the myriad things, harmonizing with all under heaven, and benefiting the hundred clans."⁴⁹

Despite apparent similarities in their attitudes toward spirit, the *Zhuangzi* and *Guanzi* have very different views of the heart-mind. They agree on the need to stabilize (*ding* 定) it. However, "Inner Workings" associates *dao* with a "mind within the mind," located in the heart-mind. And elsewhere, the *Guanzi* describes internal spirit – lodged within the heart-mind – as the ruler of the senses, a view the *Zhuangzi* pointedly rejects. In the *Zhuangzi* by contrast, spirit is concentrated through the fasting of the heart-mind.

In summary, the *Zhuangzi* seems to consistently recommend concentrating and stabilizing spirit, both in "spirit persons" and also in exemplary individuals of skill.⁵⁰ This account of realized spirit goes well beyond any kind of purely intellectual mastery.

3.3 The *Huainanzi*

Arguments that humans and spirits have the same composition and that a human can effectively become a spirit through self-cultivation practices reappear in several chapters of the *Huainanzi* (second-century BCE).⁵¹

---

⁴⁶ 雖天地之大, 萬物之多, 而唯蜩翼之知. *Zhuangzi* 19/50/14–15.
⁴⁷ 輒然忘吾有四枝形體也. *Zhuangzi* 19/52/7.
⁴⁸ 然後入山林, 觀天性; 形軀至矣, 然後成見鐻, 然後加手焉. *Zhuangzi* 19/52/7–8.
⁴⁹ 配神明, 醇天地, 育萬物, 和天下, 澤及百姓. *Zhuangzi* 33/97/21.
⁵⁰ For a fuller study of these skill masters see Lai and Qiu 2019.
⁵¹ For the background and nature of the *Huainanzi*, see Major 2003, and Puett 2002.

3.3.1 Qi, Essence, and Spirit

Like "Inner Workings," "Originating in *Dao*" (Yuandao 道原, Chapter 1) describes the physical body, *qi*, and spirit as the formative elements of a human being. Quoting *Daodejing* 41, it stresses that they all must function properly:

> The form is the residence of life; *qi* is the origin of life; spirit is the governor of life. If [even] one loses its place, then [all] three are harmed.
>
> 夫形者, 生之所也; 氣者, 生之元也; 神者, 生之制其也。一失位, 則三者傷矣. (*Huainanzi* 1/9/15–16)[52]

The passage continues that each can be destroyed or lost: the form if it inhabits an unsafe place, the *qi* if more is used than replenished, and spirit if it acts in a manner it ought not (*Huainanzi* 1/9/16–18). But for this correct alignment to take place, spirit and the body must be interdependent: spirit must control the form, and the form must provide a lodging place for spirit: "Thus, if one takes spirit as the master, the form will follow and will benefit. If one takes the form as controlling, spirit will follow and be harmed."[53] Otherwise, essence and spirit become depleted over time. Eventually, "the form closes its openings and spirit has nowhere to enter."[54] Here, spirit controls the body but, unlike texts that assert the rulership of the heart-mind – which is not mentioned in this chapter – spirit's control is effortless and not antagonistic: "Therefore sages nourish their spirits, harmonize and soften their *qi*, and pacify their forms."[55]

This and other chapters of the *Huainanzi* offer the now familiar claims that humans and spirits have the same composition and humans can become spirit-like by practicing self-cultivation techniques.

"Essence and Spirit" (*Jingshen* 精神, Chapter 7) describes the origin and nature of human beings composed of refined *qi*:

> Essence and spirit are of Heaven; bones and frame are of Earth. When essence and spirit enter its [Heaven's] gate, and the bones and frame return to their [Earth] roots, how can I still survive?
>
> 精神, 天之有也; 而骨體者, 地之有也。精神入其門, 而骨體反其根, 我尚何存? (*Huainanzi* 7/54/27–28)

Essence and spirit are necessary to survival, but tend to dissipate. The "Essence and Spirit" chapter argues that self-cultivation practices can not only retain them in the body, but that essence and spirit (*jingshén*) are the basis of sagehood.

---

[52] Translations are indebted to Major et al. 2010 and Puett 2002.
[53] 故以神為主者, 形從而利; 以形為制者, 神從而害. *Huainanzi* 1/10/3.
[54] 形閉中距, 則神無由入矣. *Huainanzi* 1/10/4–5.
[55] 是故聖人將養其神, 和弱其氣, 平夷其形. *Huainanzi* 1/10/8–9.

It begins with the origins of spirit and the body during the development of the human embryo. During gestation, yin and yang *qi* gradually acquire differentiated physical form, and a person emerges, composed of both physical form (received from Earth) and spirit (received from Heaven):

> The one generates the two; the two generate the three; the three generate the myriad things. The myriad things carry yin on their backs, embrace yang and, through the blending of qi become harmonious.
>
> 一生二, 二生三, 三生萬物。萬物背陰而抱陽, 沖氣以為和. (*Huainanzi* 7/55/7–8)

The process of ontogeny culminates in the formation of the five yin viscera: the heart, lungs, kidneys, liver, and spleen: "In the tenth month, birth occurs. In this way, the form and frame are thus complete, and the five *zang* [yin] viscera take form."[56]

The *Huainanzi* is explicit about the analogies between the human microcosm and a cosmic macrocosm. The head is round like Heaven, the feet square like earth. The four limbs, five yin viscera, nine orifices, and 366 joints of the human body correspond to Heaven's four seasons, five phases, nine regions, and 366 days. Human taking, giving, happiness, and anger correspond to Heaven's wind, rain, cold, and heat:

> Therefore, the gall bladder parallels the clouds, the lungs parallel the air, the liver parallels the wind, the kidneys parallel rain, the spleen parallels thunder. In this way they [humans] form a triad with Heaven and Earth, and the heart-mind is the ruler.
>
> 故膽為雲, 肺為氣, 肝為風, 腎為雨, 脾為雷, 以與天地相參也, 而心為之主. (*Huainanzi* 7/55/11–14)

The concern of the chapter is how to maintain the alignment of the human body relative to the cosmos. This is done through the activity of the heart-mind, but ultimately through the activity of spirit. If the heart-mind can control the five yin viscera, attention is not distracted and the movement of *qi* does not go awry. As a result, "Essence and Spirit will be abundant and *qi* will not dissipate."[57] The individual functions in accordance with underlying patterns (*li* 理) gains impartial equanimity (*jun* 均) and develops penetrating awareness (*tong* 通):

> When you have penetrating awareness, you become like a spirit. Spirit-like, your vision has nothing unseen, your hearing nothing unheard, and your actions nothing incomplete.

---

[56] 十月而生。形體以成, 五藏乃形. *Huainanzi* 7/55/9–10. See Puett 2002: 272–284.
[57] 精神盛而氣不散矣. *Huainanzi* 7/55/21–22.

> 通則神，神則以視無不見〔也〕，以聽無不聞也，以為無不成也。
> (*Huainanzi* 7/55/23–24)

The chapter then turns to "Perfected Persons" who "embody their foundation and embrace their spirit in order to wander in the confines of Heaven and Earth."[58] But they gain spirit by distancing themselves from both their bodies and their heart-minds: "Their bodies are like withered wood; their heart-minds are like dead ashes. They forget their viscera and lose their bodies."[59] Like the *Zhuangzi*'s spirit person, their spirits roam free: "They possess essence but do not give it orders; they possess spirit but do not make it move."[60]

3.3.2 The Heart-Mind

What is the role of the heart-mind in these processes? In the description of human ontogeny, it is the heart-mind that forms a triad with Heaven and Earth. But the person described here is literally a newborn child, not a realized individual.

As in the *Guanzi*, the heart-mind is essential to the process of self-cultivation because its activity is necessary for the entry of spirit. It is the heart-mind that controls the five yin viscera, ensures the correct movement and preservation of *qi*, and ensures that essence and spirit are abundant. So the heart-mind is essential to the process but is a means, not an end. As "Essence and Spirit" puts it: "The heart-mind is the ruler of the form; spirit is the treasure of the heart-mind." Part of the heart-mind's function is to guard against depletion of both the body and of essence and spirit. Just as the body can become exhausted by excess labor, if essence and spirit are used unceasingly, they too run out.[61]

The chapter goes on to contrast practitioners of what elsewhere have been called "guiding and pulling" exercises with those who cultivate the heart-mind. However, the real contrast is with those who cultivate spirit: "they make their spirit overflow and do no lose its fullness"; that is, they do not permit it to dissipate.[62]

In summary, the *Huainanzi* combines the now familiar claim that correct self-cultivation practices can give humans the powers of spirits with an account of humans as microcosms of the cosmos. As a result, self-cultivation methods can link a realized person with the patterns of the universe. This connection is accomplished through the correct cultivation and alignment of body and spirit

---

[58] 體本抱神，以游於天地之樊。*Huainanzi* 7/57/11.
[59] 形若槁木，心若死灰。忘其五藏，損其形骸。*Huainanzi* 7/57/15–16, paraphrasing *Zhuangzi* 22/61/1.
[60] 有精而不使者，有神而不(行)。*Huainanzi* 7/57/21–22.
[61] 故心者，形之主也；而神者，心之寶也。*Huainanzi* 7/57/2–3.
[62] 是養形之人也，不以滑心。使神滔蕩而不失其充。*Huainanzi* 7/58/4.

through the activity of the heart-mind. But the more spirit-like one becomes, the less the body and heart-mind come to matter.

3.4 Conclusions

We can trace a different awareness of the relation of the body and spirit through several stages. The "Inner Workings" chapter of the *Guanzi* focused on the development of internal spirit, including the role of the body in that development. Crucial to that development is essence (*jing*), which "Inner Workings" positions as the basis of physical human life, the root of sagacity, and common to both human spirit and external spirits.

In the process of lodging and refining essence to create spirit, the hear-mind serves as an intermediary by aligning the senses and providing a lodging place for essence. "Inner Workings" describes spirit as naturally present in the embodied person, but by nature something that comes and goes. It is only stabilized by a combination of correct alignment of the embodied person and the stabilizing activity of a settled mind. Once settled, it naturally aligns the senses. As a result, the adept becomes "like a spirit."

In "Inner Workings" the mind is an essential part of the self-cultivation process. In the *Zhuangzi*, by contrast, it is an obstacle. Various chapters underline the need to both "concentrate spirit" and to "fast the mind." Others praise "spirit people" and reiterate the importance of spirit (but never of mind) to the exercise of high orders of skill.

The *Huainanzi* returns to the positive use of the heart-mind in "Inner Workings but reworks these arguments in different ways. "Essence and Spirit" frames the human body as a microcosm of the cosmos and focuses on the nature of essence and spirit as the Heaven-derived components of a person. In particular, it focuses on the necessity to and means of using the heart-mind in self-cultivation practices to keep essence and spirit together.

4 Medical Texts

Most of the preceding discussion has followed understandings of body, mind, and spirit in what are conventionally referred to as "Masters" texts, and it is these texts that are often identified with early Chinese philosophical traditions. Many of these texts shared both overlapping interests and in some cases intertextuality in the sense of what may have been a common pool or reservoir of ideas and even direct quotations.[63] Self-cultivation literature is no exception,

---

[63] The term "Masters text" (*zi* 子) refers to influential texts from the Warring States and Han periods ascribed to eponymous "masters," whose disciples recorded and transmitted their teachings. See Fischer 2009.

and we find overlaps of ideas about the nature of body, mind, and spirit in Masters texts, such as the *Guanzi*, *Mengzi*, *Zhuangzi*, and *Huainanzi*. We also find the same concerns outside of Masters texts, for example, in the "Ten Questions" text from Mawangdui, and also in the *Huangdi neijing*.

The first part of this section examines the "Ten Questions" text from the medical manuscripts discovered at Mawangdui. The second part examines the treatment of the "heart" (*xin*) and spirit (*shén*) in the *Huangdi neijing*.

4.1 Ten Questions

"Ten Questions" (*Shiwen* 十問) is one of a group of broadly medical manuscripts discovered at Mawangdui, along with two versions of the *Laozi*. As Donald Harper has shown, these texts seem to be the product of a heterodox intellectual community that may have included not only the "philosophers" of the Masters text world but also the quasi-medical "recipe masters" or *fangshi* 方士, as well as non-Masters "naturalist" theories of *qi*, yin-yang 陰陽, and *wuxing* 吾行. Harper refers to this intellectual milieu as a "cross-fertilization" of Warring States medicine and philosophy.[64] As Rohan Sikri has pointed out, these overlaps do not take an explicitly interdisciplinary form (Sikri 2021: 432). We do not see, for example, explicit quotation of medical arguments by philosophers (or vice versa) as is so prominent in the Greek use of medical examples and analogies by philosophers. Instead, we find concepts across genres, without explicit interaction. Nonetheless, as Geoffrey Lloyd and Nathan Sivin point out, we find the abilities underlying (science and) medicine are diffused through many levels of Chinese society (Lloyd and Sivin 2002: 27). That diffusion includes ideas and techniques concerned with body, mind, and spirit in self-cultivation literature.

In particular, early medical texts such as those found at Mawangdui do not identify *xin* with *shén*, nor do they present the heart as distinct from the other viscera in substance or kind. In other words, they do not treat *xin* and *shén* as a mind-spirit amalgam in a dualistic scheme.[65]

Accounts of enhancing spirit by *qi* cultivation also appear in the "Ten Questions" from Mawangdui. It consists of ten questions posed on topics related to longevity that include accounts of *qi* cultivation and methods to attain

---

[64] Harper 1998: 44. For the broader context of medical writing see Harper 1999: 91–110 and 2001: 99–120. For linkages between the formation of professional groups and books that codified their professional knowledge see Li Ling 1993. For additional remarks on medicine and philosophy see Brown 2015, Lloyd and Sivin 2002, Lo 1998, and Sikri 2021.

[65] The term *xin* occurs 563 times in the *Huangdi neijing*. I focus on co-occurrences of *xin* and *shén*, and do not discuss passages where *xin* is described purely as a bodily organ (e.g., "harming the heart," "heart *qi*), the heart as a location in the body (e.g., "a disease in the heart"), or the vessels connected with the heart.

spirit illumination. The response to the first question, on how living things move and grow, recommends: "Eat yin, secure yang; attain spirit illumination."[66] Spirit illumination arises from what appear to be breath or sexual techniques, starting with a "recipe to penetrate spirit illumination." It describes a series of breath manipulations:

> Still your spirit wind, make fast your two racks, triply pound, and let nothing escape ... suck it in not more than five times, bring it to the mouth, and still it with the heart-mind.
>
> 靜而神豐，拒而兩持。三築而毋遂 ... 吸毋過五，致之口，枚之心.
> (Mawangdui 1985, 4: 145, strips 3–7, Harper 1998: 386)

The recipe is described as a method to "penetrate spirit illumination" and "a *Dao* of eating spirit qi."[67] Question 3 portrays spirit illumination as the result of what appears to be a sexual technique.[68]

Question 4 addresses longevity in an account of the gestation of the embryo during pregnancy (Harper 1998: 393n2). The response indicates techniques to accord with the cycles of Heaven and Earth, including techniques to attain *shénmíng*. It explains that those who are skilled at cultivating *qi* (*zhi qi* 治氣) and concentrating essence (*tuan jing* 摶精) accumulate the signless, and essence and spirit overflow like a fountain. The practitioner is advised to drink from the fountain and circulate its essence and spirit internally. As a result, "spirit will flow into form" (*shén nai liu xing* 神乃溜刑).[69] The result is health and longevity; the body attains a cloud-like radiance; filled with essence, it is able be long-lasting. The passage ends with the injunction that, to make the spirit long-lived (*shou shén* 壽神), it is necessary to "breathe with the skin's webbed pattern" (*yi cou li xi* 以腠理息). It continues that "the essence of cultivating *qi* (*zhi qi zhi jing* 治氣之精) is to exit from death and enter into life"; "to fill the form (*cong xing* 充形) with this [*qi*] is called concentrating essence" (*bo jing* 摶精). But there is a difficulty; essence leaks out of the body and must be supplemented.[70] This leakage can be prevented by storing up essence.[71] As a result, the practitioner becomes a spirit and is liberated from form.

"Spirit flowing into form" and procedures for filling the body with *qi* seem to be methods for extending the longevity of body and spirit through breath

---

[66] 食陰擬陽，稽於神明. *Mawangdui* 1985: 4: 145, strips 1–2, Harper 1998: 385. Citations of the *Shiwen* are from *Mawangdui Hanmu boshu* volume 4 (1985), henceforward Mawangdui 4, cited by page number and strip number.
[67] 通於神明，食神氣之道. Mawangdui 4: 145, strips 3–7, Harper 1998: 388.
[68] Mawangdui 4: 146, strips 17–18 and 22–23, Harper 1998: 390–391.
[69] Mawangdui 4: 146–147, strips 28–29, Harper 1998: 394.
[70] Mawangdui 4: 147, strips 36–39, Harper 1998: 396.
[71] Mawangdui 4: 147–148, strips 54–55, Harper 1998: 396.

exercises. There is no suggestion that they benefit the heart-mind, which is not mentioned at all.

In summary, in the "Ten Questions," *shén* is clearly linked with the body, but not to the heart-mind. In conclusion, in most of the passages discussed above, the heart-mind and spirit are discussed in different contexts. In passages where *xin* refers to some kind of mental activity, accounts of mind – and its cultivation – typically focus on rites, music, and the virtues, and do not mention spirit. Accounts of spirit occur in the quite different context of accounts of the balance and regulation of *qi*, essence, and yin and yang, and do not focus on the heart-mind.

4.2 Heart-(Mind) and Spirit in the *Huangdi Neijing*

This section focuses on the *Huangdi neijing* 黃帝內經. This work is multi-authored and especially difficult to date. Some chapters are clearly addressed to physicians in a therapeutic or diagnostic context; others are more broadly philosophical or even cosmological. Following most contemporary scholarship, I understand the *Huangdi neijing* as a multi-authored compilation of smaller units whose dates are uncertain, although much of its content is believed to date from the Han dynasty.[72] There are three known texts of the *Huangdi neijing*: the *Suwen* 素問 (Basic Questions), compiled by Wang Bing 王冰 in 762;[73] the *Lingshu* 靈樞 (Numinous Pivot), compiled in the twelfth century;[74] and the *Taisu* 太素 (Great Basis), compiled by Yang Shangshan 楊上善 in the seventh century.[75]

One way in which it seems to have had different purposes and audiences than philosophical texts is the status of the heart-mind as the center of cognition and moral judgment. Starting with the *Mengzi*, the role of the heart-mind becomes a central issue in philosophical texts, but not in medical texts. By contrast, in medical contexts such as the *Huangdi neijing*, the central role of spirit *was* the prerequisite for maintaining life and health. Nonetheless, medical writers adapted cosmologies that had elsewhere been applied to government to explain medicine. They also drew on other technical traditions, including the

---

[72] Nathan Sivin (1993: 196–215) dates the contents of the *Suwen* to the first century BCE. Paul Unschuld (2003: 1–7, 26–43, 59–65, 77–80) dates its language and ideas to between 400 BCE and 260 CE. Some content may be considerably later. See also K. Yamada 1979: 67–89 and Ma 1990.
[73] Citations from the *Suwen* are from G. Yamada 2004 (hereafter, SW). Translations are from Unschuld and Tessenow 2011, sometimes modified.
[74] Citations from the *Lingshu* are from Shibue 2003 (hereafter LS). Translations are from Unschuld 2016, sometimes modified.
[75] It is lost in Chinese editions, but is preserved in Japanese editions of the *Huangdi neijing*. See Kosoto 1981 and Sivin 1998: 29–36.

iatromantic contexts of recipe masters and diviners. Medical adaptations of these ideas in turn were incorporated into a new ideology that associated the structure of the cosmos to that of both the human body and the state (Despeux 2007: 72, Sivin 1995). The authors of the *Huangdi neijing* introduced an acupuncture-based model of the body, especially in the *Lingshu*. Its multiple accounts of *xin* and *shén* are not always consistent.

Compared to most philosophical texts, the *Huangdi neijing* presents a more decentralized and corporeal view of body-mind integration in which the heart-mind, spirit, and several other psychophysical faculties are closely integrated with various aspects of the body. In particular, *xin* – when it does not refer specifically to the heart – is the container or lodging place of spirit, rather than as the seat of consciousness and moral judgment. In this section I thus translate *xin* as "heart" when it refers to the physical organ in the body, for example, as the dwelling place of spirit, or in comparison to the lungs and liver. But as a "psychophysical" organ, the "heart" also refers to the "mind," as in other Warring States and Han texts.

The *Huangdi neijing* uses five different terms to refer to the body. There seem to be no obvious differences in meaning between these terms; in some cases several appear within a paragraph, with no apparent shift in meaning. (A full examination of this issue is beyond the scope of the present study.) Most frequent are "form" (*xing*, 305 times) and "embodied person" (*shēn*, 252 times). Less frequent is "frame" or "limbs" (*ti*, 70 times) and the compounds *shēnti* 身體 (21 times) and *xingti* 形體 (6 times).

The *Huangdi neijing* refers to the *xin* (elsewhere "heart-mind") extensively, but in most cases the term refers to the heart, one of the five yin viscera. Like the other yin viscera, it is linked to a psychological function, in this case *shén*, but with no specific emphasis on the mind or cognitive functions. It does refer to a unique role o the heart as the container of lodging place of *shén*, rather than as the seat of consciousness and moral judgment. For these reasons I focus on the uses of *shén* in the *Huangdi neijing*. It makes three important claims about the roles of *xin* and *shén* in the body. The first is the medically important claim that *shén* is the foundation of all life. Second, the five yin or *zang* 藏 viscera act as storehouses or habitations for five key psychological faculties, including *shén* (discussed in section 4.2.2).[76] Finally, emotional excess harms the five *zang*

---

[76] The *Huangdi neijing* distinguishes two kinds of viscera. Five *zang* 臟 (modern form 藏) "depots" or "treasuries" (the heart, lungs, liver, spleen, and kidneys) are concerned with transformation and storage and are considered yin. Five *fu* 腑 (modern form 府) viscera (the gall bladder, stomach, large and small intestine, urinary bladder) provide reception and passage, and are considered yang. I refer to the five *zang* viscera as the five yin viscera. See SW 4.99, Unschuld and Tessenow 2011: 1: 89.

viscera, especially the heart (*xin*), the lodging place of *shén*. These claims also involve the assertion that the heart is the ruler of the other yin viscera.

4.2.1 Spirit as the Foundation of Life

Lingshu 8 immediately asserts the importance of *shén:* "For all methods of needling, it is first necessary to consider *shén* as the foundation."[77] The text continues that the five *zang* viscera store six constituents of the body, but excess or indulgence causes them to leave the viscera. The six components are: blood (*xue* 血), the vessels (*mai* 脈), camp *qi* (*yingqi* 營氣), guard *qi* (*weiqi* 衛氣), essence (*jing*), and spirit (*shén*).[78]

The text identifies spirit with the emergence of life. By contrast, the heart-mind simply "manages things": "Therefore the origin of life is called essence; the clash of two [kinds of] essence is called *shén*. What comes and goes following spirit is called *hun*; what enters and leaves along with essence is called *po*.[79] What is responsible for things is called the *xin*."[80]

The central role of spirit in maintaining life also appears in discussions of natural lifespan. *Suwen* 1 describes the long-lived sages of highest antiquity as "able to keep form and spirit together and to exhaust their years allotted by heaven."[81] It also describes sages who did not exhaust themselves with either physical labor or reflection and worry: "their form and frame did not deteriorate and their essence and spirit did not dissipate."[82]

"The Years Allotted by Heaven" (*Tiannian* 天年, *Lingshu* 54) explicitly associates *shén* with an allotted life span, elsewhere described as "mandate" or destiny (*ming* 命). It describes the storage of *shén* in the heart as part of normal ontogeny, beginning with the developing embryo: "The [*qi* of one's] mother constitutes the basis; that of the father serves as shield. Loss of spirit results in death; those who keep spirit survive."[83] It adds that a person is only

---

[77] 凡刺之法, 先必本于神. LS 8.190, Unschuld 2016: 147.
[78] The terms "camp *qi*" (*yingqi*) and "guard *qi*" (*weiqi*) refer to "constructive" and "protective" *qi*, respectively. Both are military terms, and they refer to two types of *qi* in the body that were believed to protect it and ward off intruders. See Unschuld and Tessenow 2011: 1: 18.
[79] These two terms refer to two "souls": the *hun* 魂 or *hun*-soul (literally cloud soul) and *po* 魄 or *po*-soul (literally white soul). For the meaning of these terms see Seidel 1982, Y. Yu 1987, Brashier 1996, and Y. Lo 2008.
[80] 故生之來謂之精, 兩精相搏謂之神, 隨神往來者謂之魂, 並精而出入者謂之魄, 所以任物者謂之心. LS 8.191–195, cf. Unschuld 2016: 148–49. A commentary glosses the "two *jing*" as the essence of yin and yang. Understood thus, the interactions of yin and yang essence – the origin of life – produces *shén*, which is thus associated with the origin of life, and precedes *xin*.
[81] 能形與神俱, 而盡終其天年. SW 1.20; Unschuld and Tessenow 2011: 1:31–32.
[82] 形體不敝, 精神不散. SW 1.38; Unschuld and Tessenow 2011: 1:44. For *jing shén* as "essence and spirit" see Tessenow and Unschuld 2008: 210–211. Unschuld notes the use of *jing* in several compounds, but consistently understands *jing shén* as "essence and spirit."
[83] 以母為基, 以父為楯, 失神者死, 得神者生也. LS 54.778, Unschuld 2016: 514.

complete when: blood and *qi* are in harmony, camp and guard *qi* penetrate the body, the five yin viscera (including the heart) are complete, and spirit *qi* has settled in the heart.[84] This passage makes clear that spirit is stored in the heart as spirit *qi*, and the completion of that process is essential for the formation of a person. Life span can be limited by depletion of *qi* associated with the viscera over the course of a normal lifetime. At the age of sixty, heart *qi* starts to weaken; by eighty, lung *qi* weakens and the *po* soul departs. By one hundred, "all five *zang* are depleted, spirit *qi* entirely left" and death follows.[85]

Several *Suwen* passages discuss the importance of correct seasonal activities for preserving spirit *qi*, such as "collecting spirit *qi*" in autumn (SW 2.45, Unschuld and Tessenow 2011: 1: 48–49); and preserving it in winter (SW 3.82, Unschuld and Tessenow 2011: 1: 78). The *Suwen* also gives technical instructions for needling to preserve and balance spirit *qi* (SW 27.625 and 62.1214, Unschuld and Tessenow 2011: 1:452, and 2: 105–106).

4.2.2 Storage of Psychological Faculties

Several accounts of spirit indicate that it is stored in and associated with the heart. Some occur in fivefold correlations between the five yin viscera and five psychological faculties stored in them. Both the *Suwen* and *Lingshu* describe the yin viscera as storing five psychological faculties. According to the *Suwen*: "The heart stores spirit; the lungs store *po*; the liver stores *hun*; the spleen stores thought; the kidneys store will."[86] An almost identical passage occurs in the *Lingshu*; the only difference is that the kidneys store essence and will.[87] A different correlation occurs in *Suwen* 62, which focuses on the completion of the physical form: Here, heart stores spirit, the lungs store *qi* (instead of *po*), the liver stores blood (instead of *hun*), the spleen stores flesh (instead of thought), and the kidneys store will: "Will and thought penetrate [everything], in the interior they link up with bones and marrow, thereby completing the form of the person and the five *zang* viscera."[88] This passage undermines claims for a radical distinction between the physical body and a separate mind or consciousness because there is no clear distinction between "containers" (the yin viscera) and their contents: both psychological attributes (spirit, will) and

---

[84] 血氣已和, 營衛已通, 五藏已成, 神氣舍心. LS 54.778, Unschuld 2016: 514.
[85] 五藏皆虛, 神氣皆去. LS 54.783, Unschuld 2016: 516–518.
[86] 心藏神, 肺藏魄, 肝藏魂, 脾藏意, 腎藏志. SW 23.569–570, Unschuld and Tessenow 2011: 1: 409.
[87] 心藏神, 肺藏魄, 肝藏魂, 脾藏意, 腎藏精志也. LS 78.1070; Unschuld 2016: 735. *Lingshu* 78 (78.1056; Unschuld 2016: 727) offers a longer series of correlations between the human body and the nine regions of the cosmos.
[88] 志意通, 內連骨髓, 而成身形五藏. SW 62.1211, Unschuld and Tessenow 2011: 2:102.

"physical" attributes (qi, blood, flesh). SW 18 also describes the heart as storing *qi* (SW 18.407, Unschuld and Tessenow 2011: 1:305).

These two different accounts are reconciled in a passage in *Lingshu* 8, which describes a system of storage of both psychophysical and material aspects of a person in the five yin viscera. Each yin organ stores (*zang* 藏) a material component which "hosts" (*she* 舍) a psychological capacity. In addition deficiency or excess of the *qi* associated with each organ generates a state of strong emotion, in the following pattern:

> The heart stores the vessels; the vessels host spirit. When heart *qi* is depleted, there is grief; when it is full [excessive], there is unceasing laughter.
>
> 心藏脈, 脈舍神, 心氣虛則悲, 實則笑不休. (LS 8.200, Unschuld 2016: 152)

The full correlations are (LS 8.199–201, Unschuld 2016: 152–153):

Organ	Storage	Host	Depletion	Excess (fullness)
Liver	blood	*hun* 魂	fear	rage
Spleen	camp qi	thought (*yi* 意)	weak limbs, disordered yin viscera	distended abdomen, blocked urine and menses
Heart	vessels	spirit (*shén*)	grief	laughter
Lungs	qi	*po* 魄	blocked nose, shortness of breath	
Kidneys	essence	will (*zhi* 志)	receding qi	distension

The context appears to be diagnostic: the manifestations associated with each type of *qi* excess or deficiency can be used to diagnose the cause of the imbalance.

4.2.3 Protecting Spirit from Emotional Excess

The association of spirit with survival implies the need for therapeutic practices to protect it. Several passages focus on the emotions as a source of potential harm to spirit and therapeutic techniques for protecting and enhancing spirit.

Lingshu 8 explains in detail how emotional excess can injure spirit. It specifically correlates five key emotions with the five yin viscera and the five psychological capacities they govern. Fear (*chu* 怵), excess caution (*ti* 惕), excess reflection (*si* 思), and worry (*lü* 慮) harm spirit; when spirit is harmed, fear flows in excess and does not stop. Grief and sorrow (*bei'ai* 悲哀) exhaust the *qi* in the center and can cause death. Joy and pleasure (*xi le* 喜樂) cause spirit to scatter and disperse, so it cannot be stored. Worry and sadness (*chou you* 愁憂) cause closure and blockage of the *qi*, so it cannot move. Raging anger (*sheng nu* 盛怒) causes confusion and cannot be cured or regulated. Fear and dread (*kong ju* 恐懼) make spirit disseminate, so it cannot conserved (LS 8.195–96, Unschuld 2016: 149). As a result, those who understand how to nurture life (*yang sheng* 養生) understand how to regulate and harmonize their emotions (LS 8.194, Unschuld 2016: 149). As these passages make clear, all emotional excess is harmful, but some particularly affect the heart or spirit. When fear injures spirit, people lose their sense of self (LS 8.196–198, Unschuld 2016: 150).

4.2.4 Xin *as Ruler of the Visceral Systems*

The *Huangdi neijing* consistently describes spirit as being stored in the heart, sometimes along with statements that the heart is the ruler of the other viscera. For example, *Suwen* 8 makes an analogy between the five yin viscera and five key offices of government. Here the heart is the ruler of eleven other officials in both the yin and yang viscera: (1) lungs (minister and mentor), (2) liver (general), (3) gall bladder (rectifier), (4) dan zhong (minister and envoy), (5) spleen and (6) stomach (grain storage), (7) large and (8) small intestines (transmitter and recipient), (9) kidneys (operator with force), (10) triple burner (opener of channels), (11) urinary bladder (regional rectifier).[89] These twelve officials (including the heart) work together to maintain the life of the body, which dies if they do not perform correctly.

Claims that the heart-mind is the ruler of the body are part of dominant narrative in Warring States and Han philosophical texts such as *Guanzi*, *Mengzi*, *Xunzi*, and other texts (discussed in Section 2).[90] Similar claims in the *Huangdi neijing* stand in strong contrast to early second-century (BCE) medical texts from Mawangdui and Zhangjiashan. The *Huangdi neijing* reflects the importance of a new model of corporeal/political relations, including the need for harmony between ruler and officials (Lewis 2006: 37; Unschuld 1985: 79–83).

However, some of the *Huangdi neijing* descriptions of the heart as ruler of the other viscera seem to be in the service of something else. For example, *Lingshu* 36 describes the heart as ruler over both the other viscera, and also over the senses:

> As for the five *zang* and six *fu* viscera, the heart is the ruler: the ears are the listeners, the eyes are the observers, the lungs are the prime minister, the liver

---

[89] SW 8.237–40, Unschuld and Tessenow 2011: 1:155–158. The *Huainanzi* (1/8/9–10) also refers to the heart as the "ruler of the five *zang* viscera" (夫心者, 五藏之主也).

[90] For more on the rulership of the mind see Geaney 2002: 17–18, Raphals 2015: 132–182, Sabattini 2015: 58–74, and Unschuld 1985: 100.

is the general; the spleen is the guardian; the kidneys are the governors of the outer regions.

五藏六府, 心為之主, 耳為之聽, 目為之候, 肺為之相, 肝為之將, 脾為之衛, 腎為之主外. (LS 36.632; Unschuld 2016: 384–385)

Here the context is an explanation of the movement of fluids in the body. Liquids from the viscera normally pour into the eyes, and when the heart feels grief, they flow as tears. The point of the passage is to explain tears, not to assert the rulership of the heart. Another passage makes clear that the importance of the heart is its domicile for spirit:

> The heart is the great ruler of the five *zang* viscera and six *fu* viscera; it is where essence and spirit reside. As long as this *zang* viscera is firm and stable, evil [*qi*] cannot be permitted [entry]. If it is permitted, the heart is damaged; if the heart is damaged, spirit leaves; if spirit leaves, [the person] dies.
>
> 心者, 五藏六府之大主也。精神之所舍也。其藏堅固, 邪弗能容也。容之則心傷, 心傷則神去, 神去則死矣. (LS 71.934, Unschuld 2016: 639–640)

Here, the heart is important, not for itself but as the site of spirit, which is essential for survival.

In summary, several points are noteworthy about the heart and spirit in the *Huangdi neijing*. First, the heart is closely associated with spirit and its essential role in maintaining the life of the body. Second, the *Huangdi neijing* identifies five distinct psychological capacities associated with the heart. In these passages, there is no separation between mind and body: the material organ (e.g., the liver) cannot be detached from the *hun* stored in it. Third, these texts are striking for the extent to which they describe what in contemporary terms might be called distributed cognition by both decentralizing and "corporealizing" consciousness, effectively removing psychological control from the heart and distributing it among the viscera.

4.2.5 "Corporealizing" Consciousness

The *Huangdi neijing* repeatedly links spirit to essence (*jing*) and *qi* in the constitution of a person. Several passages combine *shén* with clearly material aspects of the body in their accounts of yin and yang, *shén*, *jing*, and *qi*. *Lingshu* 5 describes proper storage of spirit in the body as the union of corporeal form and *qi*:

> Balancing yin and yang [*qi*] causes essence *qi* to become luminous. Uniting form and *qi* causes spirit to be stored internally.
>
> 調陰與陽, 精氣乃光, 合形與氣, 使神內藏. (LS 5.158; Unschuld 2016: 123)

Here, storage of *shén* occurs through the union of the clearly corporeal *xing* and *qi*. There is no contrast between a corporeal body and a noncorporeal spirit.

Lingshu 18 also describes *shén* as a component of the body: "Camp and guard [*qi*] are essence *qi*. Blood is spirit *qi*. Hence blood and *qi* may have different names, but they are the same in kind."[91] The context is an explanation about why blood and *qi* have different names but are "the same in kind" (*tong lei* 同類). Camp and guard *qi* are defined as essence *qi* and blood as spirit *qi*. Both are identified with the physical body.

Lingshu 47, "Taking the *Zang* Viscera as the Foundation" (*Ben zang* 本藏) also describes the *zang* viscera as storing psychological faculties: "The five *zang* viscera are what stores essence, spirit, blood, *qi*, *hun* and *po*." Will and thought (*zhi yi* 志意) regulate essence, spirit, *hun*, and *po* and harmonize joy and rage. As a result, essence and spirit are focused, *hun* and *po* do not dissipate, regret and rage do not emerge, and the five *zang* viscera are protected from external invasive *qi*.[92] In this account, will and thought, psychological faculties associated with the kidneys and spleen, regulate the other psychological faculties stored in other viscera.

Two *Suwen* passages suggest some kind of spirit-body dualism in a contrast between a clearly material body and a possibly immaterial spirit. They mention four corporeal ("form") viscera (*xing zang* 形藏) and five "spirit viscera" (*shén zang* 神藏), identified with the five *yin* viscera: heart, lungs, spleen, liver, and kidneys: "Thus, the corporeal *zang* viscera are four, the spirit *zang* viscera are five. Together this makes nine *zang* viscera to correspond to them."[93] A second passage mentions that there are five spirit viscera (*shén* zang 神藏) and four "corporeal viscera" (*xing zang* 形藏).[94] Yet other than these two passing references, neither the *Suwen* nor the *Lingshu* discuss "corporeal" or "spirit" viscera, nor do they appear in two other early sources, the *Nanjing* or *Jiayi jing*. By contrast, they appear repeatedly in Tang-dynasty sources.[95] In other words, there may well be an argument for spirit-body dualism in later medical sources, but not in the *Huangdi neijing*.

In summary, in the *Huangdi neijing*, the key role of the heart (*xin*) is its role as the storehouse or dwelling of spirit (*shén*). As such, it is one of five *yin* or *zang*

---

[91] " 血者, 神氣也。故血之與氣, 異名同類焉. LS 18.441; Unschuld 2016: 265. *Shénqi* seems clearly to refer to the spirit *qi* that must settle in the heart as part of the completion of the body.
[92] 五藏者, 所以藏精神血氣魂魄者也. LS 47.706; Unschuld 2016: 448. Unschuld translates *jing shén* as "essence spirit" rather than as "essence and spirit" and *zhi yi* as "mind" rather than "will and thought."
[93] 故形藏四, 神藏五, 合為九藏, 以應之也. SW 9.251, Unschuld and Tessenow 2011: 1:168.
[94] 故神藏五, 形藏四, 合為九藏. SW 20.483, Unschuld and Tessenow 2011: 1:356.
[95] An example is Dunhuang manuscript P3477, "Xuan Gan's Pulse Canon" (*Xuan Gan mai jing* 玄感脈經). See Ma 1998: 153 and Wang 2005a: 54 and 2005b: 395.

viscera that store five psychological faculties liked to preserving health, and longevity, but *shén* is unique insofar as it is necessary for life itself. Because it is vulnerable to the injurious effects of emotions, protecting the heart and spirit from harmful emotions is essential to life, health, and longevity. In the context of the therapeutic perspective of medical texts, spirit is the basis of life and health, rather than—associated with *xin*—the locus of cognition and moral judgment, as in many philosophical texts. Thus the *Huangdi neijing* tradition reflects what may be fundamental differences of genre in treatments of the relation between *shén* and *xin* in medical, as distinct from philosophical literature. Thus *shén* is of central importance in both genres, but for different reasons.

What then do we make of accounts of *xin* as ruler of the body or the senses in medical texts? They tend to occur in accounts of the heart as the lodging place of spirit, including in fivefold correlations between viscera and psychological faculties.

4.3 Conclusion

The medical texts surveyed here are not primarily concerned with the cognitive and moral aspects of *xin* that are a major focus for philosophical texts. By contrast, medical and philosophical texts do share an interest in *shén*, as an essential element that must be protected from harm in order to ensure survival. *Shén* is also a focus for self-cultivation practices in both traditions, but the details vary considerably, both between medical and philosophical techniques and between different medical traditions.

Masters text accounts of cultivating *qi*, essence and spirit mention the balance and regulation of *qi*, the refinement and accumulation of essence, and the arrival and entry of spirit, described sometimes as spirit *qi* (shénqi) or spirit and essence (*jing shén*). By contrast, the techniques described in "Ten Questions" mention *qi*, but focus on breath manipulation and sexual techniques. The *Huangdi neijing* focuses on protecting *shén* from injury, both by external, invasive "heteropathic" *qi* (*xie qi* 邪氣) and by the influence of emotions. Protecting *shén* inherently includes protecting the heart, where it is lodged.

Many hermeneutic and textual issues complicate our understanding of both the *Huangdi neijing* and excavated medical texts. Nonetheless, there are important contrasts between "Ten Questions" and the *Huangdi neijing* in their treatment of *xin* and *shén*. In both, *shén* is the important element. However, in early medical literature such as the "Ten Questions," *xin* is not necessarily identified with *shén* and is not represented as being distinct from the other viscera as ruler of the body. In the *Huangdi neijing*, *xin* and *shén* are closely linked, and *xin* is also linked to the other four yin viscera in fivefold correlations with psychological faculties stored in them.

5 Perspectives on Embodiment

Although the mind-centered and spirit-centered texts surveyed above differ in important ways, they agree on a view of the heart-mind as embodied, and more broadly, on what in contemporary terms can be called embodied cognition. But what does this mean? Although "embodiment" is an important concept in many areas of cognitive science, opinions differ on exactly what it is, what kind of body it requires, and what kind of embodied cognition it engages in. I use the term in the sense of what he calls organismic embodiment: the view that cognition is limited to living bodies, and that cognition is what living systems do in interaction with their environment.[96] Embodied cognition refers to a diverse research program in cognitive science, linguistics, neuroscience, philosophy, and psychology, among other disciplines. It rejects the computational model of the mind of traditional cognitive science in favor of a focus on the roles of the physical body in cognition, and holds that interactions between the body and the environment constitute or contribute to cognition (Shapiro and Spaulding 2025). Both are incompatible with mind-body dualism.

Despite possible suggestions of mind-body dualism in some texts (discussed in Section 1), From roughly the third century BCE, philosophical texts overall are nondualist and understand cognition as embodied insofar as they understand human and other animate bodies as composed of and animated by *qi*. Qi was understood as being of various kinds (yin or yang, coarse or rarefied, etc. or yang). Thus, although it was animating (ore animate) and dynamic, it was always material. This point is significant because essence (*jing*) and spirit (*shén*) were understood as rarefied and hyper-rarefied forms of *qi*.[97] Thus both Chinese mind-centered and spirit-centered texts share a view that the mind is embodied. Importantly, both consider embodiment as central to their approaches to self-cultivation, but in very different ways. Awareness of the body as a site of development and power became a topic of discourse that different traditions used to articulate their own values and priorities. In mind-centered texts, an embodied mind and spirit rules and guides the body, primarily through ritual. Spirit-centered texts, including some medical texts, advocated

---

[96] This is the fifth of six senses of the term embodiment identified by Tom Ziemke (2004): (1) a "structural coupling" between agent and environment. This is not restricted to living things, (2) historical embodiment as the result of structural coupling over time, (3) physical embodiment, (4) organismoid embodiment (of organism-like entities such as a humanoid robot), (5) organismic embodiment of autopoietic, living systems, and (6) social embodiment.

[97] For useful discussions of this point see Stanley-Baker 2022 and Yang 2025: 2–4.

a range of self-cultivation practices that used the body, and in some cases the heart-mind, to engender spirit, the most refined mode of *qi*.

5.1 Mind-Centered Texts

In mind-centered texts, the heart-mind may rule the body, but its development occurs through the body, primarily through ritual, but also in accounts of the importance of music. The role of and problems with embodiment are even clearer in the *Xunzi*. According to Xunzi, people are inherently drawn toward the objects of their desires (*yu* 欲).[98] Desires are perceived through the senses, but can only be realized through the controlling activity of the heart-mind, which is inherently drawn toward profit ((*li* 利).[99] Xunzi's approach to countering these tendencies relies heavily on the embodied practice of ritual and propriety (*liyi* 禮義). In addition to the performance of group rituals such as marriages, funerals, and rituals of state, ritual governed many details of daily behavior, such as clothing, posture, and the giving and taking of everyday objects. This kind of quotidian behavior in turn affected human feelings, and through them, desires. Ritual works by modifying and improving human emotional dispositions (*qing* 情).[100] It was a way to manifest inner feelings outwardly, and in the process, to refine and channel them in socially appropriate directions.[101]

Xunzi also clearly believed that practicing virtue made the practitioner embody it: "If, with a heart–mind of integrity, you cling to benevolence, you will embody it; if you embody it, you will be a spirit; if you are a spirit, you will be able to transform things."[102] Xunzi is also explicit that ritual is necessary for self-cultivation of the heart-mind to occur: "In the arts of controlling *qi* and nourishing the heart–mind, nothing is more direct than ritual."[103] Finally, Xunzi often links ritual with music:

> Thus, when music is performed, the will becomes pure; when ritual is cultivated, conduct is perfected. The eyes and ears become clear and acute; the blood and *qi* become harmonious and even; practices are altered and customs change.[104]

---

[98] Sung 2012a: 214–215. For the question of whether desires can themselves motivate action see Sung 2012b. The hegemony of the heart-mind over the senses is discussed further in Raphals forthcoming.

[99] Xunzi 22/111/6–7 (trans. Hutton 2014: 243) and 23/114/12 (Hutton 2014: 250).

[100] He describes *qing* as "the feelings of like and dislike, of delight and anger, and of sorrow and joy that are given from birth" (22/107/22–23).

[101] This point is indebted to Sung 2012a.

[102] 誠心守仁則形, 形則神, 神則能化矣. *Xunzi* 3/11/4–5 (Hutton 2014: 19).

[103] 凡治氣養心之術, 莫徑由禮. *Xunzi* 2/6/9 (Hutton 2014: 12).

[104] 故樂行而志清, 禮脩而行成, 耳目聰明, 血氣和平, 移風易俗. *Xunzi* 20/100/7–9 (Hutton 2014: 221).

Xunzi clearly viewed ritual as a means to transform people's moral states through their physical states. It is also possible that he also viewed ritual as a response to a range of corporeal quasi-medical self-cultivation practices such as meditation, breath cultivation, gymnastic practices, and sexual practices. Many of these appear in spirit-centered texts, and as the evidence of excavated texts makes clear, these techniques were becoming increasingly popular among Warring States elites in the third century. Xunzi may have presented ritual as an alternative embodied practice for managing *qi* (as well as the mind) and providing physical and spiritual benefits (Tavor 2012, 2013).

5.2 Spirit-Centered Texts

Spirit-centered texts, including some medical texts, advocated a range of self-cultivation practices that used the body, and in some cases the heart-mind, to engender spirit, the most refined mode of *qi*, in what some scholars refer to as "biospiritual" practices.[105]

We find accounts of what we could also call "embodied spirit practices" in a wide range of early Chinese literature, including masters texts and medical literature, but also in dynastic histories and poetry, which are not discussed here. What these texts share is an understanding of self-cultivation as a progressive refinement of qi, essence, and spirit. Spirit-centered texts offer self-cultivation techniques in which the body is the site of both the stabilization of the heart-mind and the entry of spirit. This approach is very different than the ritual-centered embodied practices of mind-centered texts.

In the techniques described in the *Guanzi*, correct somatic alignment and awareness stabilizes the heart-mind and creates the essence from which spirit emerges. By contrast, some techniques in the *Zhuangzi* call for "starving" the heart-mind, but others call for making the body like a withered tree or dead ashes. The *Huainanzi* links accounts of the cultivation of essence and spirit with new claims that humans are microcosms of the cosmos, and self-cultivation practices can link a realized practitioner with the patterns of the universe.

5.3 Medical Texts

Some of the same concerns and claims appear in medical texts, albeit in a somewhat different therapeutic context. The "Ten Questions" texts from Mawangdui appear to present an interaction between medicine and philosophy in medical accounts of cultivating *qi* and attaining spirit illumination in order to attain health and longevity. The *Huangdi neijing* specifically identifies essence

---

[105] Yang 2025, citing studies by Harper 1998, Lewis 2006, Puett 2002, Raphals 2023, Roth 1999, and Slingerland 2019, though these texts do not use the term.

as the origin of life and spirit as the basis of life. Here the heart-mind is both the seat of the emotions and one of the five yin viscera. As a therapeutic text, a central concern is protecting the heart-mind and the spirit that lives in it from injury or death. Both texts, in different ways, clearly present the heart-mind as embodied. They are not directly concerned with cognition but insofar as they address it, it is clearly embodied.

6 Comparative Observations

Just as the mind-body problem is a major topic in contemporary and modern philosophy, the relation of "body and soul" – *sōma* and *psychē* – was a major topic in Classical Greek philosophy. For this reason, a few comparative observations are in order. They are tentative and warrant further study, and limitations of space preclude detailed textual references and discussion. In the Greek world as in the Chinese, simplified "mind-body" binaries ignore or misrepresent important aspects of Greek thinking. There is a danger of retrojecting contemporary views of mind and body on *psychē* and *sōma*. I conclude with a few comparative remarks.

6.1 Two Histories of Body and Soul

An important starting point is the claim that, at least in a Greek context, concepts of the soul were derived from concepts of the body. Like the rich vocabulary of Chinese terms for bodies, minds, and spirits, Greek understandings of key terms and concepts, including but not limited to *psychē* and *sōma*, were complex and polyvalent. As in China, the concept of "having" a "body" had a history. In a Greek context, Brook Holmes has shown that the body first emerges as a concept in the writings of the speculations of sixth- and fifth-century "inquirers into nature" about the ultimate constituents and causes of perceived phenomena. They developed new explanations, based on imperceptible, impersonal forces, rather than divine agencies and conceptualized these objects and forces in terms of their nature (*phusis*). Hippocratic physicians developed these ideas in texts on human nature and the nature of the body as an object of specialist medical knowledge. Fifth-century medical interest in the nature of the body was part of the broader context of the inquiry into nature, including the claim that it had a nature. The Hippocratic corpus (c.450–350 BCE) represents the body as an object of specifically technical knowledge that was necessary to care for and preserve it. These texts engage debates about nature in the specific context of human nature, including the nature of the body, especially *On the Nature of a Human Being*, *On Regimen*, and *On Ancient Medicine* (Holmes 2010a: 22–23, 990–110).

It is Plato who introduced a dualistic opposition between body and soul that is primarily focused on the soul. Even so, he retained some naturalistic accounts of the body. He reworked medico-naturalistic accounts of the care of the body into a new account of the care of the soul as the source of cognitive and ethical judgments. Elsewhere, he expressed an at least partially psychophysical medical view of the body: in the Charmides, where he asserts the need to treat the person as a whole (*Charm.* 156e7-11), in the "harmony" model introduced but rejected in the *Phaedo* (87c), and in brief mention of the need for balance between body and soul in the *Republic* (352e-353e) and *Timaeus* (88b7-c1).

Regardless of Socrates' motivations for the dualistic portrayal of body and soul in the *Phaedo*, he almost immediately shifts to the much more nuanced account of the tripartite soul of the *Republic* and later dialogues. For example, *Republic* 1 (352e-353e) describes the correct functioning of both body and soul as the correct functioning of each of its parts. However, the point of the analogy is not any interest in the function of the body but rather to justify the account of the parts of the soul. As Brook Holmes has argued, the conceptualization of the body in Greece helped motivate the conceptualization of the soul as the locus of the person (Holmes 2010a: 6–30, 2010b: 345–346, 2017: 18–20).

A Chinese history of the body takes a different course. A new understanding of the importance of the body first appears in textual fragments attributed to the fourth-century figure Yang Zhu 楊朱 (fl. ca. 370–350 BCE). Accounts of him appear in the *Mengzi*, *Lushi Chunqiu*, and *Huainanzi*, and four chapters of the *Zhuangzi* (chs. 28–31) contain what is now considered Yangist material (Graham 1989: 54–59). As Mark Lewis notes, concern over the body figures in all presentations of Yangist doctrines, and the core of Yangist teachings, was the supreme value of life and the body. "Preserving one's nature" entailed nourishing bodily energies and developing bodily powers (Lewis 2006: 17).

Doctrines ascribed to Yang Zhu appear as titles of several sections of the *Lushi chunqiu*.[106] Other passages identify "essential nature" (*xing* 性) with life (*sheng* 生, Brindley 2022). In other words, keeping one's nature intact meant preserving one's true self or what is "genuine" (*zhen* 真), but also preserving one's health, safety from danger, and living out one's natural lifespan. Yangist stories in the *Zhuangzi* and *Liezi* describe individuals rejecting rulership and power in order to preserve their health and physical wellbeing (Lewis 2006: 18–20). John Emerson argues that Yang Zhu's major innovation was the "discovery of the body," which

---

[106] "Life as Basic" (*Ben sheng* 本生, ch 1.2), "Giving Weight to Self" (*Zhong ji* 重己, ch. 1.3), "Fundamental Desires" (*Qing yu* 情欲, ch. 2.3), and "Awareness of the Purpose of Action" (*Shen wei* 審為, ch. 21.4). For discussion see Graham 1989: 55. For further discussion of Yang Zhu see Defoot and Lee 2022, Brindley 2022 especially.

redefined the relationship between the individual and the state, resulting in both a new political order and a new sense of self (Emerson 1996: 533).

As Mark Lewis notes, by the mid-Warring States period, the trope of the body and life as markers of supreme value had become conventional. This "body" was defined in spatial terms as a central self set against external objects, rather than a Western dualistic opposition between body/matter and mind or soul/spirit. The mind – or more properly the heart-mind (*xin*) – was part of the body; it was essentialized and refined, but of the same substance. Properly cultivated and protected, it could generate spirit-like powers (*shén*). This model of the body first appeared in the Yangist doctrines and was successively adopted by rivals to articulate their own positions. As Lewis puts it, the body became problematic as one spatial unit defined in opposition to others, rather than in binary oppositions between body and mind (Lewis 2006: 20).

Awareness of the body as a site of development and power became a topic of discourse that different traditions used to articulate their own values and priorities. These ideas are further developed in the spirit-centered texts described in Section 3 of the Element: the "Arts of the Mind" chapters of the *Guanzi*, the *Zhuangzi*, the *Huainanzi*, and "Ten Questions," discussed in Section 4.1. However, in the Greek world, accounts of the body became separated from and sidetracked by accounts of the soul. This division never happened in the Chinese context, where accounts of self-cultivation remained strongly psychophysical. This is a major difference.

By contrast to the later Greek history, the Homeric poems do not make a clear distinction between "mind" and "body," and the terms *psychē* and *sōma* are used primarily of the dead, not the living. As A. A. Long puts it, "living persons in Homer are bodies through and through" (Long 2014: 25). Living "bodies" consisted of limbs (*melea, guia*), and a form (*demas*). People felt emotions, deliberated, and made plans with their hearts (*kradiē* and its cognates) and used their *thumos*, *phrenes*, and *prapidēs*, but these terms also referred to organs within the body. They also had a "soul" (*psychē*) which left the body at death, but was not linked to intelligence or personality (Clarke 1999, Claus 1981, Long 2014: 26–28, 32–37, Padel 2016).

The language of the Chinese accounts of self-cultivation surveyed here is comparable to the Homeric lexicon. Both describe an embodied person (Chinese *shēn*, Homeric *sōma*), with a form (Chinese *xing*, Homeric *demas*), and a frame and limbs (Chinese *ti*, Homeric *melea, guia*). Both describe a "mind" that is both affective and cognitive (Chinese *xin*, Homeric *kradiē* and its cognates, *thumos*, *phrenes*). Both describe an animating spirit or soul that is essential for life (Chinese *shén*, Homeric *psychē*), but also important Chinese psychological faculties (*hun*, *po*, will, thought) associated with various internal organs and several Homeric "psycho-physical" organs: *menos*, *thumos*, *phrenes*, and *prapidēs*.

6.2 Which "Soul"?

The term *psychē* originally meant the part of a person that kept it alive, and this meaning is very comparable to Chines *shén*. Over time, and under the influence of Plato especially, it came to mean the essence of a person and was linked to notions of immortality. These views were propagated by Christian institutions, but were never the only, or even the prevailing, Greek view.

The term "soul" or *psychē* first appears within the complex Homeric lexicon of multiple and overlapping terms for various aspects of bodies and souls. In the sixth and fifth centuries, the term *psychē* comes to mean three very distinct clusters of concepts. The first is of *psychē* as the distinguishing feature and source of the vital functions of any living organism, which distinguishes it from inanimate objects. This is extremely comparable to a key understanding of Chinese spirit as necessary to the maintenance of life.

The second is a philosophical understanding of the *psychē* as the "self": the locus of personal identity and immortality, by which the core individual persists after death. Despite many textual difficulties surrounding Pythagoras and Orphism, there is evidence that, some two hundred years after Homer and Hesiod (about 500 BCE), beliefs about an afterlife started to circulate in which the quality of the afterlife of the *psychē* depended on the moral quality of its earlier life. In this new understanding, as Long again so elegantly puts it, is that the essence of human identity is no longer psychosomatic, but psychic (Long 2014: 69).

The third is a view of the *psychē* as the "mind," in the sense of being the mental or psychological agent who experiences both cognitive and affective states, including thought and planning, perception and desire, and as he bearer of moral qualities and as the bearer of the qualities of individual identity. (This taxonomy is informed by, but differs from, that of Lorenz 2009.) One result of this expansion is the emergence of a distinction between body and soul – which is not present in the Homeric poems. The accounts of the soul formulated and extensively discussed in the fragments of the *physiologoi* and works of Plato and Aristotle draw on these developments.

But the continued existence of a "soul" after death presupposes that whatever comprises the "core" identity of a person must survive death in some form and be attributed to the soul (Lorenz 2009: 9, cf. Barnes 1983: 103–106; Furley 1956: 11; Huffmann 2009). Plato makes key arguments for the immortality of the soul in the *Phaedo* and clearly considered the soul to be a nonphysical essence of human nature and identity that existed before birth and after death.[107] These arguments are less comparable to the Chinese evidence because accounts of Chinese spirits and ancestors are not centered on claims for the postmortem persistence of the core aspects of a person. Plato and probably the Pythagoreans are the major, and unduly influential, exception to this pattern. Starting at least with Plato and quite possibly with the Pythagoreans, Greek philosophy has tended, to borrow from Mengzi, to take the psyche as the "greater part" of a person.

Greek views of an embodied person reemerge with Aristotle and also in Stoic and Epicurean philosophy. But Platonic, dualistic concepts of the soul mark a strong divergence from both earlier Greek, and most Chinese accounts of the "care of the self" as psychophysical. Greek body–soul dualism is strongly focused on views of *psychē* as identity bearer and as the mind, or at east the "rational" part of the soul; and it largely ignores the view of *psychē* as the animating essence of living things. It is also noteworthy that this distinction is entirely absent from the Homeric poems, where the *psychē* is neither a moral agent nor an identity bearer. Chinese evidence may suggest a fresh look at that history, but that is beyond the scope of the present discussion.

6.3 Chinese and Greek Psycho-physicalism

In contrast to stereotypes of a "monist east and dualist west," I would argue that the real contrast in matters of mind-body dualism is between a dualist modernity and a psycho-physicalist antiquity, Chinese and Greek.

To make this distinction clear, let me clarify two points. First, a defining feature of post-Cartesian mind-body dualism in Western philosophical traditions is the view that agency resides in the mind, and the body's main role is to follow the mind's orders.[108] If cognition is understood as a prerogative of the mind, agency becomes correspondingly disembodied. By contrast, according to psycho-physical accounts of mind and body, such as that of Aristotle, perceptions, emotions, and desires are psycho-physical. As the Aristotelian scholar David Charles explains it, neither these activities nor their properties can be explained without reference to both physical and psychological activities, capacities, and properties. Nor can they be understood by decomposition into "two definitionally separate components, one purely psychological (defined without explicit reference to the physical), the other purely physical (defined without reference to the psychological)." Rather, for Aristotle, the

---

[107] These include the affinity argument (78b-80b), which addresses the concern that the soul is dispersed and destroyed at death and a final argument for the immortality of the soul. See Bostock 1986, Lorenz 2009: 12, and Robinson 1995: 29–30.

[108] I am grateful to Karyn Lai for comments on this point.

psychological activities involved in perception, emotions, and desires are "inextricably psycho-physical" and not definable by such decomposition. This means that it is impossible to define purely psychological features of a person independently of the physical or purely physical features or capacities independently of the psychological.[109]

As the foregoing discussion has shown, Chinese accounts of the heart-mind are strongly psycho-physical, whatever their view of the relation between *xin* and *shén*. Similarly, with the major exception of Plato and his intellectual descendants, Greek views of persons are overall more psycho-physical than dualist. We find psycho-physical accounts of persons in the Homeric poems, the fragments of the physiologoi, the Hippocratic corps, Aristotle, and Hellenistic Stoic and Epicurean philosophy, albeit differently expressed in each. Plato and probably the Pythagoreans are the major, and unduly influential, exception in their views of mind–body, or soul–body, dualism.

7 Conclusions

This Element has surveyed the complex interrelations between bodies, minds, and spirits in early Chinese psychology. Section 2 surveyed claims for the hegemony of the heart-mind across a range of Warring States and Han texts which assert the primacy of the heart-mind and its capacity to make cognitive and normative judgments. In the *Analects* and *Mengzi* it guides and regulates desires; the *Xunzi* introduces a new focus on its cognitive capacities. These texts describe the primacy of heart-mind over the body or senses, often in metaphors that compare the mind to the ruler of a state. In some texts, this hegemony arises not from the heart-mind itself but from spirit, which inhabits it. Here, the heart-mind and spirit function more as an amalgam than as two separate but interacting faculties. The result is a binary view of a person in two senses: a separation between the body and mind or spirit, and the agency of the heart-mind-spirit amalgam as the ruling and active part of the polarity, with the body as ruled and passive. Both are consistent with mind-body dualism.

Section 3 explored a very different arrangement of body, heart-mind and spirit in the *Guanzi*, *Zhuangzi*, and the *Huainanzi*, especially the chapter titled "Inner Workings." They focus on the concentration of essence (*jing*) as part of the development of internal spirit. These processes crucially involve the body

---

[109] Charles 2024: 3 and 5. Charles argues (2024: 2) that Aristotle's approach to the understanding of mind and body differed from all the currently prevailing post-Cartesian approaches to the mind-body problem, which he describes as reductionist and non-reductionist materialism, defining the psychological by causal roles, pan-psychism and neutral monism. These approaches view events as purely physical, purely psychological, or a combination of purely psychological and purely physical types.

and offer the practitioner spirit-like powers. In "Inner Workings" the heart-mind is an essential part of the self-cultivation process. In the *Zhuangzi*, by contrast, it is at times an obstacle, hence the latter's recommendations to "concentrate spirit" and "fast the heart-mind." The "Essence and Spirit" chapter of the *Huainanzi* frames the body as a microcosm of a cosmos in which essence and spirit must be kept together and retained.

Section 4 discussed two medical texts that are unconcerned with cognitive and moral aspects the heart-mind. They are fundamentally concerned with spirit as vital to life itself, and also key to health and longevity. These texts also describe self-cultivation procedures based on the balance and regulation of essence, *qi*, and spirit. In the Mawangdui text "Ten Questions" the cultivation of essence, *qi* and spirit leads to health and longevity, without involvement of the heart-mind. The *Huangdi neijing* associates spirit with the heart, both as the container in which it dwells, and as the co-ruler of the other yin viscera. The underlying medical reason for the importance of spirit is that *shén* is the basis of life.

Despite their differences, all three groups of texts present a highly corporealized view of persons as bodies, minds, and spirits, in which spirit is closely linked to essence and *qi*, and body and spirit are not easily distinguished. Taken together they suggest a nuanced position on the issue of mind–body dualism that allows for at least "soft" dualism (the view that mind and body are distinct, but are not separate substances), but also recognizes important ways in which humans *are* psychophysical, embodied beings who do not simply "think" with "minds." In addition, the very brief survey of Greek views in Section 5 also suggests that in Greek, as in Chinese antiquity, most views of human psychology were non- or weakly dualist. The real contrast seems to be between early Chinese and Greek views, and Cartesian mind–body dualism.

The psychology of early Chinese philosophical texts presents an important alternative to post-Cartesian mind–body dualism, both in the "mind-centered" and "spirit-centered" varieties discussed here. Their emphases are very different, but both link self-cultivation to the management and refinement of *qi* and describe agency in terms of the complex mutual influence of intention and *qi*.

Such post-Cartesian mind–body dualism is unimaginable for the authors of the Chinese texts described here because it is simply impossible to detach the heart-mind or spirit from the body in any of these texts. How could one separate the intentions – following *Mengzi* – from the *qi* they command? How – in the *Huangdi neijing* – could one separate spirit from a body that physically dies if spirit dissipates?

In summary, a range of modern and contemporary western accounts of personal identity are predicated on the unstated assumption of the separability of body and soul/brain. That separability simply doesn't work with ontologically continuous models, grounded in accounts of *qi* that make such claims for separability problematic in early China. The same point is also applicable to a long and nuanced history of Greek and Western views of the separability of the soul from the body.

According to the psychologist Raymond Gibbs, the legacy of a dualist Western intellectual tradition has led to a historical denial of the role of the body in thought, regarding the body as a material object infused with a nonmaterial "self" and "mind." But according to Gibbs, embodiment affects personhood at three distinct levels: neural events, the cognitive unconscious, and phenomenological experience.[110] In a contemporary context, Cartesian assumptions are being challenged by the emerging discipline of embodied cognition, which underscores how the body affects the mind.[111] Embodied cognition spans a wide range of disciplines and methodologies, but most agree that cognition is not the sole prerogative of the mind and that somatic experience, sensorimotor capacities, and the environment shape cognition in important ways. Embodied experience is fundamental to perception, concepts, mental imagery, memory, reasoning, cognitive development, language, emotion, and consciousness.[112]

Contemporary theories of embedded cognition seem compatible with early Chinese psychology.[113] Both challenge dualist models of mind and body. The corporealized mind–body–spirit boundary in early China has implications for self-awareness. The terms "self-awareness" and "self-consciousness" traditionally referred to an "internal" awareness of a "mental" self, without reference to somatic awareness. Texts across the early Chinese ideological spectrum suggest a different, corporeal understanding of self-awareness and a more complex understanding of the interrelations between body, mind and spirit.

---

[110] Gibbs 2005: 3–10. Another account of somatic cognition comes from neuroscience and the growing literature on the concept of interoception: the representation of the internal states of an organism. See W. G. Chen et al. 2021: 3.

[111] Lawrence Shapiro (2011: 4) defines cognition as embodied when it deeply depends on an agent's physical body, and (non-brain) somatic aspects play significant causal or physically constitutive roles in cognition.

[112] For example, Lakoff and Johnson (1980, 1999) argue that metaphors reflect embodied experience. Varela, Thompson and Rosch's (2016) concept of enaction to emphasize that experience of the world arises from mutual interactions between an organism's physiology, sensorimotor apparatus, and environment. For other examples see Gallagher 2005, Johnson 2017; and Menary 2010. For overview see Shapiro 2014 and Shapiro and Spaulding 2025.

[113] Karyn Lai (2019) has argued that the explanatory frameworks and perspectives of embodied cognition theory can help explain the views on knowledge and action and many important elements of mastery in the Zhuangzi skill stories from a very different viewpoint than the dominant epistemological frameworks in Western philosophy.

References

Ames, Roger T. (1993) "On Body as Ritual Practice." In Thomas. Kasulis, Roger T. Ames, and Wimal Dissanayake, eds., *Self as Body in Asian Theory and Practice*. Albany: State University of New York Press, pp. 149–156.

Ames, Roger T. (1984) "The Meaning of the Body in Classical Chinese Philosophy." *International Philosophical Quarterly*, 24(1), 39–54.

Anon. (2011) "Embodiment and Embodied Cognition." Oxford Bibliographies online. *Psychology*. Oxford University Press. https://doi.org/10.1093/obo/9780199828340-0023.

Barnes, Jonathan (1983) *The Presocratic Philosophers*. London: Routledge & Kegan Paul.

Barnes, Jonathan (ed.) (1991) *The Complete Works of Aristotle*. Princeton. 4th printing. Original printing 1984.

Bostock, David (1986) *Plato's Phaedo*. Oxford: Clarendon Press.

Brashier, Ken E. (1996) "Han Thanatology and the Division of Souls." *Early China*, 21, 125–158.

Bremmer, Jan N. (1983) *The Early Greek Concept of the Soul*. Princeton: Princeton University Press.

Brindley, Erica (2009) "'The Perspicuity of Ghosts and Spirits' and the Problem of Intellectual Affiliations in Early China." *Journal of the American Oriental Society*, 129(2), 215–236.

Brindley, Erica (2010) *Individualism in Early China: Human Agency and the Self in Thought and Politics*. Honolulu: University of Hawaii Press.

Brindley, Erica (2022) "Deconstructing 'Hedonism' Understanding Yang Zhu in the *Liezi*." In Carine Defoot and Ting-mien Lee, eds., *The Many Lives of Yang Zhu: A Historical Overview*. Albany: State University of New York Press, pp. 105–132.

Brown, Miranda (2015) *The Art of Medicine in Early China: The Ancient and Medieval Origins of a Modern Archive*. New York: Cambridge University Press.

Chan, Alan K. L. (2002) "A Matter of Taste: Qi (Vital Energy) and the Tending of the Heart (Xin) in Mencius 2A2." In Alan K. L. Chan, ed., *Mencius: Contexts and Interpretations*. Honolulu: University of Hawaii Press, pp. 42–71.

Chan, Shirley (2009) "The Ruler/Ruled Relationship in the 'Black Robes' Contained in the Newly Excavated Guodian Bamboo Texts." *Journal of Asian History*, 1(43), 19–30.

Chan, Shirley (ed.) (2019) *Dao Companion to the Excavated Guodian Bamboo Manuscripts*, Dao Companions to Chinese Philosophy 10. Dordrecht: Springer.

Charles, David (2024) *The Undivided Self: Aristotle and the Mind-Body Problem*. Edinburgh: University of Edinburgh Press.

Chen, Guying 陳鼓應 (2006) *Guanzi sipian quanshi: Jixia Daojia daibiao zuo jiexi* 管子四篇詮釋: 稷下道家代表作解析 [Guanzi's Four Interpretations: An Analysis of the Jixia Daoist Masterpieces]. Beijing: Shangwu yinshguan.

Chen, Wen G., Dana Schloesser, Angela M. Arensdorf, Janine M. Simmons, Changhai Cui, Rita Valentino, et al. (2021) "The Emerging Science of Interoception: Sensing, Integrating, Interpreting, and Regulating Signals within the Self." *Trends in Neurosciences*, 44(1), 3–16.

Chiu, Wai Wai (2016) "Zhuangzi's Idea of 'Spirit': Acting and 'Thinging Things' without Self-assertion." *Asian Philosophy*, 26(1), 38–51.

Clarke, Michael (1999) *Flesh and Spirit in the Songs of Homer: A Study of Words and Myths*. Oxford: Oxford University Press.

Claus, David B. (1981) *Toward the Soul: An Inquiry into the Meaning of Psychē before Plato*. New Haven: Yale University Press.

Cook, Scott. (2012). *The Bamboo Texts of Guodian: A Study and Complete Translation*. 2 volumes. Ithaca: Cornell University Press.

Csikszentmihalyi, Mark (2005) *Material Virtue Ethics and the Body in Early China*. Leiden: Brill.

Damasio, Antonio R. (1994) *Descartes' Error: Emotion, Reason, and the Human Brain*. New York: Putnam.

Damasio, Antonio R. (2010) *Self Comes to Mind: Constructing the Conscious Brain*. New York: Pantheon.

Defoort, Carine and Ting-mien Lee (eds.) (2022) *The Many Lives of Yang Zhu: A Historical Overview*. Albany: State University of New York Press.

Despeux, Catherine (2007) "Âmes et animation du corps: La notion de shen dans la médecine chinoise antique." *Extrême-Orient Extrême-Occident*, 29, 71–94.

Ding, Sixin 丁四新 (2006) "Shangbo Chu jian 'Gui Shen' pian zhu shi" 上博楚简《鬼神》篇注释 [Notes on the Shanghai Museum Chu bamboo strip texts "Ghosts and Gods"]. www.bsm.org.cn/show_article.php?id=337.

Ding, Sixin 丁四新 (2011) "A Study on the Dating of the Mozi Dialogues and the Mohist View of Ghosts and Spirits." *Contemporary Chinese Thought*, 42(4), 39–87.

Emerson, John (1996) "Yang Chu's Discovery of the Body." *Philosophy East and West*, 46(4), 533–566.

Fingarette, Herbert (1972) *Confucius: Secular as Sacred*. New York: Harper Torchbooks.

Fingarette, Herbert (2008) "Discovering the Analects." In David Jones, ed., *Confucius Now: Contemporary Encounters with the Analects*. Chicago: Open Court, pp. 1–12.

Fischer, Paul (2009) "Intertextuality in Early Chinese Masters-Texts: Shared Narratives in Shi Zi." *Asia Major*, 22(2), 1–34.

Fraser, Chris (2016) *The Philosophy of the Mozi: The First Consequentialists*. New York: Columbia University Press.

Fraser, Chris (2020) *The Essential Mozi: Ethical, Political, and Dialectical Writings*. Oxford: Oxford University Press.

Fraser, Chris (2024) *Zhuangzi: The Complete Writings*. Oxford: Oxford University Press.

Furley, David (1956) "The Early History of the Concept of Soul." *Bulletin of the Institute of Classical Studies, University of London*, 3, 1–18.

Gallagher, Shaun (2005) *How the Body Shapes the Mind*. Oxford: Oxford University Press.

Gassmann, Robert H. (2011) "Coming to terms with dé 德: The deconstruction of 'virtue' and an exercise in scientific morality." In Richard King and Dennis Schilling, eds., *How Should One Live? Comparing Ethics in Ancient China and Greco-Roman Antiquity*. Berlin: De Gruyter, pp. 92–125.

Geaney, Jane. (2002). *On the Epistemology of the Senses in Early Chinese Thought*. Honolulu: University of Hawaii Press.

Gibbs, Raymond W. (2005) *Embodiment and Cognitive Science*. Cambridge: Cambridge University Press.

Goldin, Paul (2003) "A Mind–Body Problem in the Zhuangzi?" In Scott Cook, ed., *Hiding the World in the World: Uneven Discourses on the Zhuangzi*. Albany: State University of New York Press, pp. 226–247.

Goldin, Paul (2015) "The Consciousness of the Dead as a Philosophical Problem in Ancient China." In Richard A. H. King, ed., *The Good Life and Conceptions of Life in Early China and Græco-Roman Antiquity*. Berlin: De Gruyter, pp. 59–92.

Graham, Angus C. (1978). *Later Mohist Logic, Ethics and Science*. Hong Kong: Chinese University Press.

Graham, Angus C. (1981) *Chuang-Tzu: The Inner Chapters*. London: Unwin Paperbacks.

Graham, Angus C. (1985) "Divisions in Mohism Reflected in the Core Chapters of Mo-tzu." In Institute of East Asian Philosophies Occasional Paper and Monograph Series 1. Singapore: Institute of East Asian Philosophies.

Graham, Angus C. (1989) *Disputers of the Tao: Philosophical Argument in Ancient China*. LaSalle: Open Court.

Guanzi 管子 (2001). In *A Concordance to the Guanzi* (管子逐字索引), eds. D. C. Lau and Chen Fangzheng. ICS Series. Hong Kong: Commercial Press.

Guo, Jue (2011) "Concepts of Death and the Afterlife Reflected in Newly Discovered Tomb Objects and Texts from Han China." In Amy Olberding and P. J. Ivanhoe, eds., *Mortality in Traditional Chinese Thought*. Albany: State University of New York Press, pp. 85–115.

Guodian Chumu zhujian 郭店楚墓竹簡 (1998). [Bamboo Slips from the Chu Tombs at Guodian]. Beijing: Wenwu.

Harper, Donald J. (1998) *Early Chinese Medical Literature: The Mawangdui Medical Manuscripts*. London: Keegan Paul International.

Harper, Donald J. (1999) "Physicians and Diviners: The Relation of Divination to the Medicine of the Huangdi neijing (Inner Canon of the Yellow Thearch)." *Extreme-Orient, Extreme- Occident*, 21, 91–110.

Harper, Donald J. (2001) "Iatromancy, Diagnosis, and Prognosis in Early Chinese Medicine." In Elisabeth Hsu, ed., *Innovation in Chinese Medicine*. Cambridge: Cambridge University Press, pp. 99–120.

Holmes, Brooke (2010a) *The Symptom and the Subject: The Emergence of the Physical Body in Ancient Greece*. Princeton: Princeton University Press.

Holmes, Brooke (2010b) "Body, Soul, and Medical Analogy in Plato." In J. Peter Euben and Karen Bassi, eds., *When Worlds Elide: Classics, Politics, Culture*. New York: Rowman & Littlefield, pp. 345–385.

Holmes, Brooke (2017) "The Body of Western Embodiment: Classical Antiquity and the Early History of a Problem." In Justin E. H. Smith, ed., *Embodiment: a History*. Oxford: Oxford University Press, pp. 17–49.

Huainanzi 淮南子, in *A Concordance to the Huainanzi* (淮南子逐字索引), eds. D. C. Lau, Ho Che Wah, and Chen Fong Ching. ICS Series. Hong Kong: Commercial Press, 1992.

Huangdi neijing lingshu 黃帝內經靈樞. See Shibue Chūsai 澀江抽齋 (2003).

Huangdi neijing suwen 黃帝內經素問. See Yamada Gyōkō 山田業廣 (2004).

Huffmann, Carl A. (2009) "The Pythagorean Conception of the Soul from Pythagoras to Philolaus." In Dorothea Frede and Burkhard Reis, eds., *Body and Soul in Ancient Philosophy*. Berlin: De Gruyter, pp. 21–43.

Hutton, Eric L. (2014) *Xunzi* 荀子 *The Complete Text*. Princeton: Princeton University Press.

Johnson, Mark (1993) *Moral Imagination: Implications of Cognitive Science for Ethics*. Chicago: University of Chicago Press.

Johnson, Mark (2017) *Embodied Mind, Meaning, and Reason: How Our Bodies Give Rise to Understanding*. Chicago: University of Chicago Press.

Jullien, F. (2007) *The Propensity of Things: Toward a History of Efficacy in China*, trans. J. Lloyd. New York: Zone Books.

Keightley, David N. (1978) "The Religious Commitment: Shang Theology and the Genesis of Chinese Political Culture." *History of Religions*, 17(3/4), 211–225.

Keightley, David N. (1998) "Shamanism, Death, and the Ancestors: Religious Mediation in Neolithic and Shang China (ca. 5000–1000 B.C.)." *Asiatische Studien /Etudes Asiatique*s, 52(3), 763–828.

Knoblock, John (1988, 1990, 1994) *Xunzi: A Translation and Study of the Complete Works*. 3 vols. Palo Alto: Stanford University Press.

Kosoto, Hiroshi 小曽戶洋 (1981) *Tōyō igaku zempon sōsho* 東洋醫學善本叢書. 8 vols. Osaka: Tōyō igaku kenkyūkai.

Lai, Guolong (2005) "Death and the Otherworldly Journey in Early China as Seen through Tomb Texts, Travel Paraphernalia, and Road Rituals." *Asia Major*, 18(1), 1–44.

Lai, Guolong (2015) *Excavating the Afterlife: The Archaeology of Early Chinese Religion*. Seattle: University of Washington Press.

Lai, Karyn, and Wai Wai Chiu (2019) *Skill and Mastery: Philosophical Stories from the Zhuangzi*. London: Rowman & Littlefield International, 143–162.

Lai, Karyn (2019) "The Cicada Catcher: Learning for Life." In Karyn Lai and Wai Wai Chiu, eds., *Skill and Mastery: Philosophical Stories from the Zhuangzi*. London: Rowman & Littlefield International, pp. 143–162.

Lakoff, George and Mark Johnson (1980) *Metaphors We Live By*. Chicago: University of Chicago Press.

Lakoff, George and Mark Johnson (1999) *Philosophy in the Flesh: The Embodied Mind and its Challenge to Western Thought*. New York: Basic Books.

Lau, D. C. (1984) *Mencius*. Bilingual ed. Hong Kong: Chinese University Press.

Lau, D. C. (1992) *The Analects*. Bilingual ed. Hong Kong: Chinese University Press.

Lee, Janghee (2005) "The Notion of Xin." Chapter in *Xunzi and Early Chinese Naturalism*. Albany: State University of New York Press, pp. 33–56.

Lewis, Mark E. (2006) *The Construction of Space in Early Chin*a. Albany: State University of New York Press.

Li, Ling 李零 (1993) *Zhongguo fangshu kao* 中國方術考 [A study of the occult arts of China]. Beijing: Zhonghua shuju.

Li, Xueqin 李學勤 (ed.) (2018) Qinghua daxue cang Zhanguo zhujian (8) 清華大學藏戰國竹簡 (捌) [The Tsinghua University Warring States Bamboo Strips: volume 8]. Shanghai: Zhongxi shuju.

Liu, Zhao 劉釗 (2003) *Guodian Chujian xiaoshi* 郭店楚簡校釋 [An Interpretation with Corrections of the Guodian Chu Slips]. Fuzhou: Fujian Renmin Chubanshe.

Lloyd, Geoffrey E. R and Nathan Sivin (2002) *The Way and the Word: Science and Medicine in Early China and Greece*. New Haven: Yale University Press.

Lo, Vivienne (1998) "The Influence of Yangsheng 養生 Culture on Early Chinese Medical Theory." Ph.D. Dissertation, School of Oriental and African Studies, University of London.

Lo, Yuet-Keung (2003) "Finding the Self in the *Analects*: A Philological Approach." In Kim Chong Chong, Sor-hoon Tan, and C. L. Ten, eds., *The Moral Circle and the Self : Chinese and Western Approaches*. Chicago: Open Court, pp. 249–268.

Lo, Yuet- Keung (2008) "From a Dual Soul to a Unitary Soul: The Babel of Soul Terminologies in Early China." *Monumenta Serica*, 56, 23–53.

Long, A. A. (2014) *Greek Models of Mind and Self*. Cambridge, MA: Harvard University Press.

Lorenz, Hendrik (2009) "Ancient Theories of Soul." *The Stanford Encyclopedia of Philosophy* (Summer 2009 ed.), ed. E. N. Zalta http://plato.stanford.edu/archives/sum2009/entries/ancient-soul/.

Lunyu 論語 [Analects] (1995). In *A Concordance to the Lunyu* (論語逐字索引), eds. D. C. Lau, Ho Che Wah, and Chen Fong Ching. ICS Series. Hong Kong: Commercial Press.

Ma, Chengyuan 馬承源 (ed.) (2005) *Shanghai bowuguan cang Zhanguo Chu zhushu* 上海博物館藏戰國楚竹書, vol. 5 [The Warring States Chu Bamboo Texts Collected by the Shanghai Museum, vol. 5]. Shanghai: Shanghai guji chubanshe.

Ma, Jixing 馬繼興 (1990) *Zhongyi wenxian xue* 中醫文獻學 [Study of Chinese Medical Texts]. Shanghai: Shanghai kexue jishu.

Ma, Jixing 馬繼興 et al. (1998) *Dunhuang yiyao wenxian jijiao* 敦煌醫藥文獻輯校 [The Dunhuang medical texts edited and collated]. Nanjing: Jiangsu guji.

Major, John S. (2003). *Heaven and Earth in Early Han Thought: Chapters Three, Four, and Five of the Huainanzi*. Albany: State University of New York Press.

Major, John S., Sarah A. Queen, Andrew Seth Meyer, and Harold D. Roth (trans.) (2010) *The Huainanzi: A Guide to the Theory and Practice of Government in Early Han China*. New York: Columbia University Press.

Mawangdui Hanmu boshu 馬王堆漢墓帛書 [The Silk Manuscripts from the Han Tombs at Mawangdui] (1985) Volume 4, edited Mawangdui Hanmu boshu zhengli xiaozu 馬王堆漢墓帛書整理小組 [the Mawangdui Han tombs Silk Manuscripts editorial group]. Beijing: Wenwu.

Menary, Richard (ed.) (2010) *The Extended Mind: Life and Mind*. Philosophical Issues in Biology and Psychology Series. Cambridge, MA: MIT Press.

Mengzi 孟子 in *A Concordance to the Mengzi (*孟子逐字索引*)*, edited by D. C. Laut, Ho Che Wah, and Chen Fong Ching ICS series. Hong Kong: Commercial Press, 1995.

Padel, Ruth (2016) *In and Out of the Mind: Greek Images of the Tragic Self*. Princeton: Princeton University Press.

Perkins, Franklin (2009) "Motivation and the Heart in the Xing zi ming chu." *Dao: A Journal of Chinese Philosophy*, 8, 117–131.

Poo, Mu-chou (1998) *In Search of Personal Welfare: A View of Ancient Chinese Religion*. Albany: State University of New York Press.

Puett, Michael J. (2002) *To Become a God: Cosmology, Sacrifice, and Self-Divinization in Early China*. Cambridge, MA: Harvard University Press.

Raphals, Lisa (2015) "Body and Mind in Early China and Greece." *Journal of Cognitive Historiography*, 2(2), 132–182.

Raphals, Lisa (2019) "Body and Mind in the Guodian Manuscripts." In Shirley Chan, ed., *Dao Companion to the Excavated Guodian Bamboo Manuscripts*. Dordrecht: Springer, pp. 239–257.

Raphals, Lisa (2020) "Body, Mind, and Spirit in Early Chinese Medicine." *T'oung- pao*, 106(5–6), 525–551.

Raphals, Lisa (2023) *Body, Mind, and Spirit in Early China*. Oxford: Oxford University Press.

Raphals, Lisa (forthcoming) "Thinking and Cognition in Xunzi and Aristotle." In Winnie Sung, ed., *Works of Philosophy and Their Reception: The Xunzi*. Berlin: De Gruyter.

Rickett, W. Allyn (1985, 1998) *Guanzi: Political, Economic and Philosophical Essays from Early China*, 2 vols. Princeton: Princeton University Press.

Robinson, Howard (2017) "Dualism." *The Stanford Encyclopedia of Philosophy* (Fall 2017 Edition), Edward N. Zalta (ed.), https://plato.stanford.edu/archives/fall2017/entries/dualism/.

Robinson, T. M. (1995) *Plato's Psychology*. Toronto: University of Toronto Press.

Rosemont, Henry, Jr. and Roger T. Ames (2016) *Confucian Role Ethics: A Moral Vision for the 21st Century?* Global East Asia Vol. 5. Gottingen: V&R Unipress GmbH.

Roth, Harold (1990) "The Early Taoist Concept of Shen: A Ghost in the Machine?" In Kidder Smith, ed., *Sagehood and Systematizing Thought in* the Late Warring States and Early Han. Brunswick: Bowdoin College, pp. 11–32.

Roth, Harold (1999) *Original Tao: Inward Training (Nei-yeh) and the Foundations of Taoist Mysticism*. New York: Columbia University Press.

Sabattini, Elisa (2015) "The Physiology of 'xin' (Heart) in Chinese Political Argumentation: The Western Han Dynasty and the Pre-imperial Legacy." *Frontiers of Philosophy in China*, 10(1), 58–74.

Schofield, Malcolm (1991) "Heraclitus' Theory of Soul and its Antecedents. In Stephen Everson, ed., *Psychology*. Cambridge: Cambridge University Press, pp. 13–34.

Seidel, Anna (1982) "Tokens of Immortality in Han Graves." *Numen*, 29(1), 79–122.

Shapiro, Lawrence (2011) *Embodied Cognition*. Oxford: Routledge.

Shapiro, Lawrence (ed.) (2014) *Routledge Handbook of Embodied Cognition*. Oxford: Routledge.

Shapiro, Lawrence and Shannon Spaulding (2025) "Embodied Cognition," *The Stanford Encyclopedia of Philosophy* (Summer 2025 ed.), Edward N. Zalta & Uri Nodelman (eds.), https://plato.stanford.edu/archives/sum2025/entries/embodied-cognition/.

Shibue, Chūsai 澁江抽齋 (2003) *Lingshu jiangyi* 靈樞講義 [Notes on the Numinous Pivot]. Cui Zhongping et al., ed. Beijing: Xueyuan [LS].

Shun, Kwong-loi (1997) *Mencius and Early Chinese Thought*. Stanford: Stanford University Press.

Sikri, Rohan (2021) "The Dialectics of Yangsheng: Healing by Argument in the Zhuangzi." *Philosophy East and West*, 71(2), 431–450.

Sivin, Nathan (1993) "Huang ti nei ching 黃帝內經." In Michael Loewe, ed., *Early Chinese Texts: A Bibliographical Guide*. Berkeley: University of California Press, pp. 196–215.

Sivin, Nathan (1995) "State, Cosmos, and Body in the Last Three Centuries B.C." *Harvard Journal of Asiatic Studies*, 55(1), 5–37.

Sivin, Nathan (1998) "On the Dates of Yang Shang-shan and the Huang-ti nei ching t'ai su." *Chinese Science*, 15, 29–36.

Slingerland, Edward T. (2003a) *Confucius Analects with Selections from Traditional Commentaries*. Indianapolis: Hackett.

Slingerland, Edward T. (2003b) *Effortless Action: Wu-wei as Conceptual Metaphor and Spiritual Ideal in Early China*. Oxford: Oxford University Press.

Slingerland, Edward T. (2013). Body and Mind in Early China: An Integrated Humanities–Science Approach. *Journal of the American Academy of Religion*, 81(1): 6–55.

Slingerland, Edward T. (2016) "Interdisciplinary Methods in Chinese Philosophy: Comparative Philosophy and the Case Example of Mind-body Holism." In Sor-Hoon Tan, ed., *The Bloomsbury Research Handbook of Chinese Philosophy Methodologies*. London: Bloomsbury, pp. 323–351.

Slingerland, Edward T. (2019) *Mind and Body in Early China: Beyond Orientalism and the Myth of Holism*. Oxford: Oxford University Press.

Slingerland, Edward T. and Maciej Chudek (2011) "The Prevalence of Mind–Body Dualism in Early China." *Cognitive Science*, 35(5), 997–1007.

Snell, Bruno (1953) *The Discovery of the Mind: The Greek Origins of European Thought*. Cambridge: Cambridge University Press, rpt. 1982.

Sommer, Deborah (2008) "Boundaries of the 'Ti' Body." *Asia Major*, 3rd Series, 21(1), 293–324.

Stanley-Baker, Michael (2022) "Qi 氣: A Means for Cohering Natural Knowledge." In Vivienne Lo and Michael Stanley-Baker, eds., *Routledge Handbook of Chinese Medicine*. Milton: Taylor & Francis, pp. 23–50.

Sterckx, Roel (2007) "Searching for Spirit: Shen and Sacrifice in Warring States and Han Philosophy and Ritual." *Extrême-Orient Extrême-Occident*, 29, 23–54.

Sung, Winnie (2012a) "Ritual in the Xunzi: A Change of the Heart/Mind." *Sophia* 51, 211–226. https://doi.org/10.1007/s11841-012-0313-5.

Sung, Winnie (2012b) "Yu 欲 in the Xunzi: Can Desire by Itself Motivate Action." *Dao* 11:369–388.

Tavor, Ori (2012) *Embodying the Way: Bio-spiritual Practices and Ritual Theories in Early and Medieval China*. PhD dissertation, University of Pennsylvania.

Tavor, Ori. (2013) "Xunzi's Theory of Ritual Revisited: Reading Ritual as Corporal Technology." *Dao : A Journal of Comparative Philosophy*, 12(3), 313–330.

Tessenow, Hermann, and Paul U. Unschuld. (2008). *A Dictionary of the Huang Di Nei Jing Su Wen*. Berkeley: University of California Press.

Unschuld, Paul U. (1985) *Medicine in China: A History of Idea*s. Berkeley: University of California Press.

Unschuld, Paul U. (2003) *Huang Di nei jing su wen: Nature, Knowledge, Imagery in an Ancient Chinese Medical Text*. Berkeley: University of California Press.

Unschuld, Paul U. (2016) *Huang Di nei jing ling shu: The Ancient Classic on Needle Therapy: The Complete Chinese Text with an Annotated English Translation*. Berkeley: University of California Press.

Unschuld, Paul U. and Hermann Tessenow (2011) *Huang Di nei jing su wen: An Annotated Translation of Huang Di's Inner Classic – Basic Questions*. 2 vols. Berkeley: University of California Press.

Varela, Francisco, Evan Thompson, and Eleanor Rosch (2016) *The Embodied Mind: Cognitive Science and Human Experience*. Cambridge, MA: MIT Press.

Wang, Shumin (2005a) "A General Survey of Medical Works Contained in the Dunhuang Medical Manuscripts." In Vivienne Lo and Christopher Cullen, eds., *Medieval Chinese Medicine: The Dunhuang Medical Manuscripts*. New York: RoutledgeCurzon, pp. 45–58.

Wang, Shumin (2005b) "Appendix 2: Abstracts of the Medical Manuscripts from Dunhuang." In Vivienne Lo and Christopher Cullen, eds., *Medieval Chinese Medicine: The Dunhuang Medical Manuscripts*. New York: RoutledgeCurzon, pp. 374–434.

Wong, David B. (1991) "Is There a Distinction between Reason and Emotion in Mencius?" *Philosophy East and West*, 41(1), 31–44.

Wong, David B. (2002) "Reasons and Analogical Reasoning in Mengzi." In Liu Xiusheng and Philip J. Ivanhoe, eds., *Essays on the Moral Philosophy of Mengzi*. Indianapolis: Hackett, pp. 187–220.

Wong, David B. (2024) "Zhuangzi on Not Following the Leader." *Journal of Global Ethics* 20 (3): 279–292.

Wu Kuang-ming (1997) *On Chinese Body Thinking: A Cultural Hermeneutics*. Leiden: Brill.

"*Xin shi wei zhong*" 心是謂中 [The Heart-Mind Is What Is Called the Center] (2018). In Li, Xueqin 李學勤, ed., *Qinghua daxue cang Zhanguo zhujian* (8) 清華大學藏戰國竹簡 (捌) [The Tsinghua University Warring States Bamboo Strips: volume 8]. Shanghai: Zhongxi shuju, pp. 87–90 and 148–152.

Xunzi 荀子 in *A Concordance to the Xunzi* (荀子逐字索引), eds. D. C. Lau, Ho Che Wah, and Chen Fong Ching ICS series. Hong Kong: Commercial Press, 1996.

Yamada. Gyōkō 山田業廣 (2004) *Suwen cizhu jishu* 素問次注集疏 [Collected Anotations on the Basic Questions]. Cui Zhongping 崔仲平 et al., eds. Beijing: Xueyuan chubanshe [SW].

Yamada, Keiji (1979) "The Formation of the Huang-ti Nei-ching." *Acta Asiatica*, 36, 67–89.

Yang, Chris (2025) "A Vital Matter: Essence 精, Spirit 神, and Self-Cultivation in Early China," PhD dissertation, Brown University.

Yang, Rubin 楊儒賓 (ed.) (1993) *Zhongguo gudai sixiang shi zhong de qi lun yu shenti guan* 中國古代思想史中的氣論與身體觀 [Theories of Qi and the Body in the History of Early Chinese Thought]. Taipei: Juliu tushu gongsi.

Yang, Rubin 楊儒賓 (1999) *Rujia shenti guan* 儒家身體觀 [Confucian Views of the Body]. Taipei: Zhongyang yanjiyuan zhong guo wen zhe yanjiusuo chou bei chu.

Yu, Ning (2007) "Heart and Cognition in Ancient Chinese Philosophy." *Journal of Cognition and Culture*, 7, 27–47.

Yu, Ying-Shih (1987) "O Soul, Come Back! A Study in the Changing Conceptions of the Soul and Afterlife in Pre- Buddhist China." *Harvard Journal of Asiatic Studies*, 47(2), 363–395.

Zhang, Zailin 張再林 (2008) *Zuo wei shenti zhexue de Zhongguo gudai zhexue* 作爲身體哲學的中國古代哲學 [Traditional Chinese Philosophy as the Philosophy of the Body]. Beijing: Zhongguo shehui kexue chubanshe.

Zhuangzi 莊子 in *A Concordance to the Zhuangzi* (莊子逐字索引), eds. D. C. Lau, Ho Che Wah and Chen Fong Ching. ICS series. Hong Kong: Commercial Press, 2000.

Ziemke, Tom, Richard Alterman, and David Kirsh (2004) "What's That Thing Called Embodiment?" *Proceedings of the 25th Annual Cognitive Science Society*. Psychology Press, pp. 1305–1310.

Ziporyn, Brook (2020) *Zhuangzi: The Complete Writings*. Indianapolis: Hackett.

Acknowledgment

This research was supported by a Committee on Research Grant from the University of California Riverside. It is also indebted to several earlier publications, especially Raphals 2023 and 2020, and to the colleagues whose comments and critique aided those earlier endeavors. In addition, I wish to acknowledge very helpful comments by Erica Brindley and by an anonymous reviewer from Cambridge University Press. Finally, this Element is dedicated to Gopal Sukhu (1949–2024), whose death makes this world a poorer place.

Ancient East Asia

Erica Fox Brindley
Pennsylvania State University

Erica Fox Brindley is Professor and Head in the Department of Asian Studies at Pennsylvania State University. She is the author of three books, co-editor of several volumes, and the recipient of the ACLS Ryskamp Fellowship and Humboldt Fellowship. Her research focuses on the history of the self, knowledge, music, and identity in ancient China, as well as on the history of the Yue/Viet cultures from southern China and Vietnam.

Rowan Kimon Flad
Harvard University

Rowan Kimon Flad is the John E. Hudson Professor of Archaeology in the Department of Anthropology at Harvard University. He has authored two books and over 50 articles, edited several volumes, and served as editor of Asian Perspectives. His archaeological research focuses on economic and ritual activity, interregional interaction, and technological and environmental change, in the late Neolithic and early Bronze Ages of the Sichuan Basin and the Upper Yellow River valley regions of China.

About the Series

Elements in Ancient East Asia contains multi-disciplinary contributions focusing on the history and culture of East Asia in ancient times. Its framework extends beyond anachronistic, nation-based conceptions of the past, following instead the contours of Asian sub-regions and their interconnections with each other. Within the series there are five thematic groups: 'Sources', which includes excavated texts and other new sources of data; 'Environments', exploring interaction zones of ancient East Asia and long-distance connections; 'Institutions', including the state and its military; 'People', including family, gender, class, and the individual and 'Ideas', concerning religion and philosophy, as well as the arts and sciences. The series presents the latest findings and strikingly new perspectives on the ancient world in East Asia.

Cambridge Elements

Ancient East Asia

Elements in the Series

Violence and the Rise of Centralized States in East Asia
Mark Edward Lewis

Bronze Age Maritime and Warrior Dynamics in Island East Asia
Mark Hudson

Medicine and Healing in Ancient East Asia: A View from Excavated Texts
Constance A. Cook

The Methods and Ethics of Researching Unprovenienced Artifacts from East Asia
Christopher J. Foster, Glenda Chao and Mercedes Valmisa

Reconstructing the Human Population History of East Asia through Ancient Genomics
E. Andrew Bennett, Yichen Liu and Qiaomei Fu

Archaeological Studies on Gender in Early East Asia
Mandy Jui-man Wu and Katheryn M. Linduff

Environmental Foundations to the Rise of Early Civilisations in China
Yijie Zhuang

Self and Body in Early East Asian Thought
Mark Edward Lewis

Institutions and Environment in Ancient Southern East Asia (3000 BCE to 300 CE)
Maxim Korolkov

Mind and Psychology in Early China
Lisa Raphals

A full series listing is available at: www.cambridge.org/EAEA

For EU product safety concerns, contact us at Calle de José Abascal, 56–1°,
28003 Madrid, Spain or eugpsr@cambridge.org.

www.ingramcontent.com/pod-product-compliance
Lightning Source LLC
LaVergne TN
LVHW011856060526
838200LV00054B/4361